Jean Bowring's
N·E·W
CAKE DECORATING
B·O·O·K

Jean Bowring's
N·E·W
CAKE DECORATING
B·O·O·K

ANGUS
& ROBERTSON
PUBLISHERS

ANGUS & ROBERTSON PUBLISHERS

Unit 4, Eden Park, 31 Waterloo Road,
North Ryde, NSW, Australia 2113, and
16 Golden Square, London W1R 4BN,
United Kingdom

First published in Australia
by Angus & Robertson Publishers in 1969
First published in the United Kingdom
by Angus & Robertson (UK) Ltd in 1969
Reprinted 1970, 1971, 1972, 1973, 1976,
1977, 1978, 1980 (twice), 1982
This edition 1985
Reprinted 1986

Copyright © Jean Bowring 1969

ISBN 0 207 14996 8

Printed in Singapore

Contents

*I wish to thank
the Herald and Weekly Times Ltd
for permission to use
many black and white photographs
from* Australian Home Beautiful
*in this book,
and for all the colour illustrations.
I also wish to thank Mr George Thorburn
of John F. Renshaw and Co.,
Melbourne, who modelled the
animal shapes for the
photographs in the almond
artistry section.*

Preface

If you are interested in the presentation of food as well as in cooking
you will know how much satisfaction there is in
icing and decorating a cake.

Cake icing is an art that can be learnt at home and, as this book will
show, it can be done without elaborate or expensive equipment.
But, like other crafts, it needs constant practice
if you are to develop skill, and the beginner, to avoid disappointment
and frustration, should study the first part of the book and
become proficient in all branches of pipework
before she attempts to ice a cake.

During the last few years we have seen changes in the style and design
of iced cakes, particularly wedding cakes:
where once these were fussy, and decorated on every inch of the surface,
today they more often follow the simple but elegant line of
the modern bride's wedding dress.
The same applies to birthday and other special-occasion cakes, and
because of this trend towards simplicity the amateur who
wants to ice and decorate her own cakes can feel
confident of success.
The designs given here are all practical and easy to follow and can be
adapted to suit the standard the cake decorator has reached.

Whether you create a design of your own or use those illustrated in
this book, practise the techniques, carefully follow
the necessary instructions, be patient with the handwork —
and you will have hours of enjoyment with a
fascinating hobby.

Jean Bowring

Metric Conversion Table

Oven Temperatures

The dials on some ovens are marked in degrees Celsius (centigrade); this corresponds to Fahrenheit and gas markings as follows:

Temperature	°C	°F	British Gas Marks
very cool	120	250	½
very cool	140	275	1
cool	150	300	2
warm	160	325	3
moderate	180	350	4
fairly hot	190	375	5
fairly hot	200	400	6
hot	220	425	7
very hot	230	450	8
very hot	250	475	9
very hot	260	500	9

Liquids

The standard metric unit is the litre (l), i.e. 100 decilitres (dl), or 1 000 millilitres (ml). The Imperial pint (20 fl. oz) measures slightly more than half a litre (approx. 575 ml). The American pint (16 fl. oz) measures about half a litre (approximately 500 ml).

Metric	Imperial (approx.)
30 ml	1 fl. oz
60 ml	2 fl. oz
90 ml	3 fl. oz
100-125 ml	4 fl. oz
150 ml	5 fl. oz
175 ml	6 fl. oz
200 ml	7 fl. oz
225-250 ml	8-9 fl. oz
1 000 ml (1 litre)	35 fl. oz (1¼ pints)
	(or 33½ American fl. oz)

Spoons

The tablespoon has different values in different countries. The current standard British tablespoon holds 17.7 ml, the American 14.2 ml, the Australian 20 ml, and the South African 12.5 ml.
Throughout this book the former Australian Imperial standard tablespoon of 20 ml has been used.
The current standard teaspoon in all the above countries holds 5 ml.

Weights

The metric unit is the kilogram (kg), which equals 1 000 grams (g) or approximately 2 lb 4 oz.

Metric	Imperial (approx.)
30 g	1 oz
60 g	2 oz
90 g	3 oz
100-125 g	4 oz
150 g	5 oz
175 g	6 oz
200 g	7 oz
225 g	8 oz
250 g	9 oz
275 g	10 oz
300 g	11 oz
325-350 g	12 oz
375 g	13 oz
400 g	14 oz
425 g	15 oz
450 g	16 oz (1 lb)
700 g	1 lb 8 oz
900 g	2 lb
1 kg	2 lb 4 oz

Lengths

The yard of 36 in. is slightly shorter than the metre (m), i.e. 100 centimetres (cm) or 1 000 millimetres (mm).

Metric	Imperial (approx.)
5 mm	¼ in.
10 mm (1 cm)	½ in.
2 cm	¾ in.
2.5 cm	1 in.
3 cm	1¼ in.
4 cm	1½ in.
5 cm	2 in.
10 cm	4 in.
20 cm	8 in.
30 cm	12 in. (1 ft)
91.5 cm	36 in. (1 yd)
100 cm (1 m)	39 in.

Icing Equipment

Apart from special icing tubes and screws, and perhaps a few icing "nails", the home cake decorator will require very little extra in the way of equipment than she already has in her kitchen.

If a special hobby is to be made of cake decorating, it is recommended that the bowls and wooden spoons and a glazing brush and watercolour brush should be kept apart just for the purpose, so as to ensure that they are clean and free from grease, which could mar the finished work.

Here is a list of the equipment needed (following which some information is given concerning some of the items listed):

A set of icing tubes and at least two screws
Icing bags, or sheets of strong white paper for making paper icing cones
Earthenware or glass mixing bowls
Wooden spoons
Icing nails
A pair of scissors
A spatula
A fine pointed watercolour brush
A pastry brush or a flat brush 1½ inches wide, for glazing
A fine-mesh sieve
A rolling-pin
Covers for the mixing bowl
Food colourings
Some thin white cardboard
Templates
A pair of compasses
An icing turntable (optional)
A roll of thick cotton wool
Gold and silver paper
Cake boards
Icing clippers

Essential equipment for cake decorating

Mixing Bowls

A set of three or four china or glass mixing bowls will be ample. These should range from about 5 to 9 inches in diameter. China or glass is preferred to metal or plastic because acetic acid is sometimes used in royal icing and has been known to stain a metal or plastic bowl and to discolour the icing.

Wooden Spoons

Always mix icing with a wooden spoon, preferably one with a large bowl—the icing beats up more quickly and more efficiently when a large spoon is used.

Avoid leaving the wooden spoon standing in the icing when you are not actually working with it: as soon as the icing has been mixed, remove the spoon and wash and dry it. Never use wooden spoons intended for icing in general cookery—fatty or greasy substances could be absorbed by the spoon and spoil the icing.

Icing Nails

These special flat, plastic-topped nails are for flower-making and they are available in shops that sell icing equipment. If they are unprocurable in your district you can improvise by attaching a small square of waxed paper to the end of the handle of a wooden spoon, using a dab of royal icing. The flower is piped onto this paper.

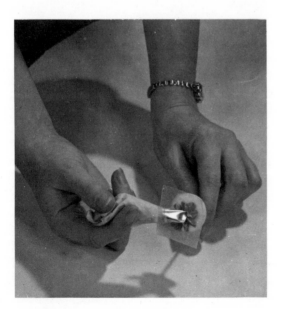

Scissors

Keep a pair of scissors in your icing kit: you'll need them when covering boards, to cut paper for icing bags, and for cutting out paper scallops to use as pattern guides when decorating a cake.

Spatula

A spatula or palette knife with its broad, pliable blade and straight edge will be useful in smoothing the glacé icing over a cake.

Watercolour Brushes

One or two watercolour brushes will be useful for adjusting fine pipework, for easing softened icing into flooded shapes, and for colouring marzipan fruits or the deeper coloured moulded or piped flowers.

Pastry Brush

This is needed when you are covering a cake with almond paste: you use it to brush the surface with jam before the paste is applied, and to lightly glaze the paste with egg white before it in turn is covered with fondant icing. The brush should be kept exclusively for cake decorating work. A small flat brush about an inch and a half wide makes a good substitute if you haven't a proper pastry brush.

Sieve

A fine-mesh sieve is a most necessary part of your icing kit. See that the mesh is free from breaks, because even one small lump in the icing could clog the tube.

Rolling-pin

This is needed for the preparation of both almond paste and fondant icing as well as for rolling out the dry icing sugar.

Covers for Mixing Bowl

Plastic covers fitted with elastic will keep the icing soft while you work, preventing a crust from forming on top, but a damp cloth or piece of thin sponge placed over the bowl is just as good.

Thin Cardboard

Thin pieces of white cardboard, with slits about a quarter of an inch in depth round the edge, are useful for holding sugar roses when you remove them from the wooden toothpicks on which they have been piped. This cardboard is also used to make templates.

Templates

A template is a pattern used to mark out a design. A simple template for cake decorating work is made from thin white cardboard in this way:

Draw an 8-inch square on the cardboard. Mark off the centre on all four sides, then draw lines from corner to corner and from the centre of each side. With a pair of compasses mark circles outward from the centre and one inch apart. Pierce the template at the junction of every line and mark two or three sets of scallops on the circle.

Have templates ready in several sizes, to save time when preparing a design for the top of a cake.

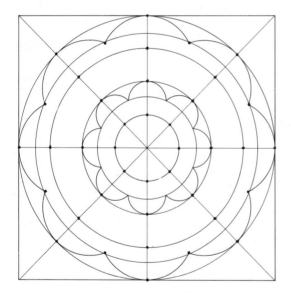

A Pair of Compasses

These are indispensable to the cake decorator. They are used in measuring, for marking dividing sections before piping a design on top of a cake, and for marking cardboard or paper templates.

Icing Turntable

If you intend doing a great deal of cake decorating, a commercially manufactured turntable is recommended. These are available in various designs and range in price from a fairly expensive one which allows the cake to be tilted (for decorating the sides) to a very simple and inexpensive one made of tin. Failing this, the home cake decorator may use a revolving savoury platter, or a large cake tin upturned on a larger tin (such as a biscuit tin) will serve the purpose temporarily.

Cotton Wool

Keep a roll of thick cotton wool exclusively for cake icing work. It is useful for holding flooded shapes in position while the icing is drying, and will protect the icing on the side of a cake should it have to be turned over and laid on its side on a flat surface (as in the Pram Cake).

Cake Boards

It is usual to have the cake board at least 2 inches larger all round than the un-iced cake, to allow for the almond and fondant icing and for the piped edge. For wedding cakes the boards vary in size from 6 inches larger than the bottom tier of the un-iced cake to about one inch larger for the middle and top tiers. Boards made of plywood may be purchased from a general hardware store, or from a timber merchant's where they will be cut to the required size. Masonite also makes good cake boards.

Extras

These include a dressmaker's inch tape, a 16-inch ruler, paper pins or drawing pins, a bottle of gum paste, and a packet of wooden toothpicks to hold icing-sugar roses. A pick board is handy for piped roses. It consists of a piece of board such as a chopping board, drilled with holes at regular intervals apart and about one-eighth of an inch deep. When piped onto the wooden toothpicks the roses are dried on the picks in an upright position on this board.

THE ICING TUBES AND BAGS

It is not necessary to purchase a large number of icing tubes to begin with. For the designs in this book you will require a minimum of seven

3

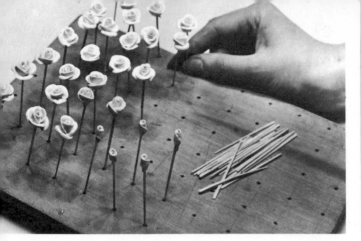

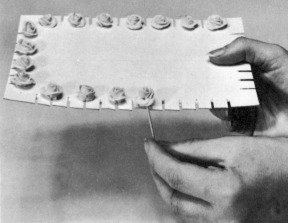

The pick board: with a small drill or a gimlet make holes not more than ⅛ inch deep in a piece of board, to hold piped roses while they are drying.

Removing piped roses from picks

tubes and you should become proficient with these before investing in any more.

Metal tubes are more satisfactory than plastic. When buying them examine each one carefully. See that no solder has been left in lumps on the inside of the tube: this could impede the free flow of the icing. Inspect the join running down the length of the tube, making sure it is secure, and see that the openings are cleanly cut and smooth.

Some icing tubes may be purchased without screw attachments; but, though they are light to handle and in some cases easier to control, they are only suitable for use in paper cones. The screw type is best, firstly because it may also be used in the paper cone and secondly because when used with the waterproof icing bag all you have to do to change the pattern is to replace the existing tube with the one you need. Some icing tubes are available for either right or left-handed work.

There are two kinds of metal tubes available in Australia: the short one of English manufacture and the more slender type made in Australia. The numbers vary according to the manufacturer, but as a guide you could buy these:

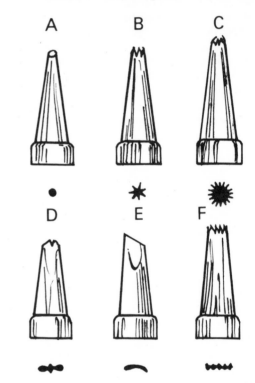

A, Writing pipe. B, Small star pipe. C, Large star pipe. D, Leaf pipe. E, Petal pipe. F, Basket-weave pipe.

Care of Tubes

Wash the icing from the tubes while it is still soft, using a feather or a small watercolour brush to clean the crevices. Never use anything with a sharp metal point (such as a skewer) to clear the icing from a tube. Instead, soak it in warm water for a short time, then use the feather or the water-colour brush to clear it.

Type of Tube	Australian number	English number
Writing tube	Nos 00, 0, 1 and 2	Nos 1 and 2
Leaf tube	Nos 16 and 17	No. 10
Petal tube	No. 20	Nos 18 and 36
Basket tube	No. 22	No. 38
Star tube	Nos 5, 8 and 12	Nos 8 and 12

Making a Paper Icing Bag

Icing bags of fairly strong white semi-glazed paper do not require an icing screw and are popular with many cake decorators. An opening large enough for the tip of the icing tube to come through is cut from the pointed end of the paper, the tube is placed in the paper cone, and the icing is spooned into the cone.

A paper icing bag may be used without a metal tube when the design would normally call for the use of a fine writing tube—for instance, lattice, line work, forget-me-nots, a flooded bell, a key, or lace appliqué. But make sure you have a well-made bag, because this is the only way you will get perfectly finished line work.

Don't use waxed paper to make the bag: it is not strong enough to take the pressure when the icing is being forced through the opening. Don't make the bag of plastic film either, because it will stretch under pressure.

If you are unable to buy the correct icing paper for the bag use a medium thick greaseproof paper or a pliable vegetable parchment.

Here's what you do to make a paper icing bag:

Take a piece of paper $8\frac{1}{2}$ inches square and cut it diagonally to make two right-angled triangles. Each triangle will make one bag. Hold the paper with the longest side (A—B) in a vertical position. Hold the middle of this edge, M, with the first finger and thumb of the right hand. Take the top corner, A, and bring it down to meet C, twisting to make a cone.

Holding corners A and C firmly, take the bottom corner, B, between the thumb and fingers of the right hand and lift it up so that the three corners (A, B and C) lie on top of one another. Holding them firmly together, fold them over, securing them in position to a depth of about one inch.

Using scissors, snip off the pointed end to make the desired size opening.

Though the paper cone is used mainly for line or string work, it is possible to cut the tip in such a way that a number of designs can be produced. For instance, a tiny leaf shape, much smaller than can be had in the metal tube range, may be made. Flatten the tip of the paper bag that is to hold the icing and, using scissors, cut a small inverted V shape (sketch A). The point of this will give the centre vein of the leaf. To make a larger leaf, cut the same type of V shape, but make it larger, then cut another V in the centre

(sketch B). For a star effect, cut the end of the bag in a straight line, then cut a W shape by nicking with scissors (sketch C).

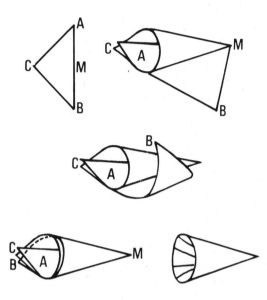

Making a paper icing bag

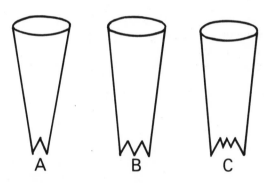

A, Paper cone cut to produce a tiny leaf shape. B, Point cut for a larger leaf. C, Point cut to give a star effect.

Making a Waterproof Icing Bag

Thin waterproof sheeting makes the conventional icing bag to take an icing screw, but one of the best materials is jaconet. It can usually be purchased in the manchester departments of the larger stores, but if you can't get jaconet don't buy a heavy twill material instead—it will be too bulky to handle. A quarter of a yard of jaconet will make three bags.

Cut the material into three 9-inch squares. Fold each one into a triangle and machine-stitch twice down one side. With scissors cut a small piece from the point of each bag, just enough to take the screw.

Attaching the screw to the bag. Turn the bag inside out and place the icing screw in the opening that was cut in the point of the bag: the thread of the screw should be inside the bag.

Using a piece of fine strong thread or string, tie the bag securely to the screw. Cut off any ends of string. Turn the bag back to its right side ready to hold the icing.

The Icings

You will need to know how to make three basic types of icing if you want to ice and decorate cakes. One is the undercoat, usually referred to as the almond icing or almond paste. The second is the covering icing, which is the rolled or fondant icing (this icing also makes moulded flowers and leaves). The third is the royal icing, which is used for all pipework and flower-making.

There is also a modelling paste or icing that sometimes replaces fondant for modelling fruit and flowers, as well as a simple glacé icing used for covering sponge sandwiches, plain butter cakes and little cakes such as petit-fours.

UNDERCOAT OR ALMOND ICING

This forms a foundation or undercoat on a rich fruit cake for a birthday, christening or wedding and it serves two purposes: it provides a smoother and more even surface for the final covering and it adds to the richness and flavour of the cake. But because it makes the cake more expensive it can be dispensed with altogether and only the covering fondant used. Or a cheaper mixture —a mock almond paste made with similar ingredients to the fondant icing—may replace it. This contains coconut and almond essence and it can also be used for coating petit-fours before the final glacé icing is added (for this purpose it should be very thinly rolled).

Because almond icing contains a percentage of almond oil (from the ground almonds that make up the mixture), which could stain and spoil the appearance of the finished cake, it is advisable to apply it at least two or three days before covering with the fondant—longer, if possible, especially for wedding cakes. However, if your time is limited, the almond layer may be brushed with unbeaten egg white or dissolved gelatine and allowed to stand until dry: either of these will form a film over the almond icing that will prevent the oil seeping through.

Miniature fruit and vegetable shapes or small animal and bird shapes may be moulded from this type of icing, but it is not suitable for moulding flowers.

> 1 lb. sifted icing sugar
> ½ lb. ground almonds
> 2 egg yolks
> ½ teaspoon lemon juice
> 2 tablespoons sherry

Sift the icing sugar into a mixing bowl and add the ground almonds. Mix until evenly blended. Beat the egg yolks with the lemon juice and sherry and stir into the sugar and almonds, mixing to a rather dry dough. Turn onto a board lightly dusted with sifted icing sugar and knead only until the icing is smooth on the outside.

Roll to the shape and size required.

MOCK ALMOND PASTE

This mock almond paste makes a more economical undercoating, especially for a child's cake.

> 1 lb. icing sugar
> ½ cup coconut
> 2 oz. liquid glucose
> 1 level tablespoon butter
> 1 egg white
> 1 teaspoon almond essence

Sift the icing sugar into a mixing bowl and add the coconut. Soften the glucose over boiling water and mix with the butter, which has been melted, and the egg white. Make a bay in the centre of the icing sugar mixture, add the glucose and butter mixture and stir, gradually drawing the dry ingredients into the centre to make a stiff paste. Flavour with the almond essence.

Turn onto a board dusted with sifted icing sugar and knead until a smooth consistency is obtained.

Use as you would almond paste, as an undercoating for fondant icing on large cakes or for the undercoat to glacé icing on petit-fours.

FONDANT ICING

This icing is simple to make and easy to use. It gives a smooth, even surface to the cake and may be tinted as desired by working in a few drops of vegetable colouring.

The fondant may be bought ready made—it is equally as good as the home-made mixture. Should you find it a little on the soft side, turn it onto a board dusted with sifted icing sugar and knead in as much icing sugar as needed to make it the correct consistency. The commercial mixture comes in 1-lb. packets and is usually known as "soft" icing.

1 lb. icing sugar
2 oz. liquid glucose
1 egg white
Flavouring and colouring

Sift the icing sugar into a mixing bowl. Soften the glucose over boiling water. Make a bay in the centre of the icing sugar and add the softened glucose, egg white and flavouring. Beat, drawing the icing sugar into the centre to make a stiff paste.

Turn onto a board lightly dusted with sifted icing sugar and knead into a paste.

If only one colour is required it may be added with the glucose and egg white, but if more than one colour is to be made from the one quantity of paste, divide after kneading and add with the tip of a skewer, then knead the colour evenly into the paste.

ROYAL ICING

Royal icing is made from pure icing sugar mixed with egg white and it is the only icing suitable for the more elaborate pipework and sugar-flower making. Only the best and purest icing sugar should be used for this icing, and it must be thoroughly sieved before it is mixed with the egg white. Inferior icing sugar or unsifted icing sugar containing even the smallest lumps can clog the icing tubes and cause delays and poor work. Poor quality icing sugar is often not pure white, which is particularly undesirable when one is making a wedding cake. On no account use what is known as icing sugar mixture for making royal icing. Such a mixture contains a percentage of cornflour to keep it soft, but the cornflour prevents the icing from holding its shape when piped. If you are in doubt, try this test: place a teaspoon of the icing sugar in a glass of cold water and allow it to settle. If the water appears clear the icing sugar is pure. Cloudy water indicates the presence of cornflour. Because pure icing sugar tends to form lumps very easily,

it should be sifted twice through a fine sieve before it is combined with the egg white. In this book "one quantity of royal icing" means one quantity as given in the following recipe, which calls for one egg white:

1 egg white
4 to 6 oz. pure icing sugar
A few drops of acetic acid or a squeeze of lemon juice

Sift the icing sugar at least twice through a fine sieve. Place the egg white in a bowl and beat until soft peaks form. Add the sifted icing sugar a spoonful at a time, beating well after each addition.

Hand beating with a wooden spoon rather than beating with an electric mixer is recommended for royal icing. The mechanical beater tends to introduce too much air into the icing, giving a false idea of its consistency. Work the icing well with the wooden spoon, adding a few drops of acetic acid or a light squeeze of lemon juice to give greater elasticity.

To overcome any slight creaminess in colour, a few drops of ordinary washing blue may be added to the icing. To make liquid blue for this purpose dilute a little solid washing blue with the lemon juice instead of with water.

When the icing is of the correct consistency for piping, tint it to the required colour, then cover the bowl with a damp cloth; keep it covered while the icing is not in use.

It is advisable to mix only as much royal icing as will be needed for the one day's piping. Should you have to keep the icing overnight, place it in a screw-topped jar or a plastic container and store in the refrigerator, then next day transfer the icing to a mixing bowl, cover with a damp cloth and let it stand until it reaches room temperature. Beat well before placing it in icing bags.

Covering the Cake

TO COVER WITH ALMOND PASTE

Place the cake on a flat, clean board. If it has risen slightly in the centre or is otherwise not a good shape, trim or level it with a broad-bladed knife, shaving rather than slicing. Use a dry pastry brush to brush away any crumbs. If you want a perfectly flat surface—this is sometimes called for in a wedding cake or a novelty cake—turn the cake upside down to ice it. Otherwise fill in any cracks in the top surface with small pieces of almond paste or fondant icing. Remember that the final icing will take the contours of the cake, so be sure you have the surface right before applying the paste or the fondant.

To make sure that the icing clings, the surface of the cake must be brushed with a glaze. This can be a specially made syrup, or apricot jam thinned down with a little hot water and then rubbed through a sieve, or you can use unbeaten egg white.

To make the syrup glaze place one tablespoon each of water, sugar, and liquid glucose in a small saucepan and stir till the sugar has dissolved and the mixture is smooth. Boil for one or two minutes. Let it cool down before use.

The syrup or the jam is recommended for the almond paste covering, and either the syrup glaze or the egg white for the fondant.

Rolling the Icing

Sift some icing sugar onto a pastry board and dust your rolling-pin with icing sugar. Roll the almond paste into either a square or a round shape, depending on the shape of the cake. In size it should be slightly less than the overall measurement of the top and sides of the cake. (It will drop a little when it is smoothed over the cake.) Roll the paste or icing round the rolling-pin and lift it carefully onto the cake.

Having dusted your hands with sifted icing sugar smooth the covering gently over the cake with your palms. Should any air bubbles appear in the icing (they will show as lumps), prick them with a pin and then gently smooth the icing again.

Lift the cake onto a covered board and trim the surplus icing away from the base, using a broad-bladed sharp knife. Leave for several days before covering with fondant icing.

TO COVER WITH FONDANT ICING

Whether you use an undercoat of almond paste on a rich fruit cake or not is a matter of personal taste and of cost. If you dispense with it you must make the fondant coat a little thicker. It will take almost 2 lb. of fondant to completely cover a $\frac{1}{2}$-lb. butter-weight fruit cake (that is, one baked in an 8-inch round or square cake tin).

If the cake has risen in the centre, level it off with a broad-bladed knife. Brush away the crumbs (they will spoil the appearance if they are allowed to become mixed with the icing).

Any cracks or uneven spots on the surface of the cake should be filled in with small pieces of fondant.

Dust the rolling-pin and pastry board with sifted icing sugar or cornflour. Roll the fondant into a round or a square shape, depending on the shape of the cake. The rolled-out fondant should measure slightly less than the overall measurement of the top and sides of the cake. Brush the surface of the cake with egg white. Roll the fondant icing round the rolling-pin, then carefully lift onto the cake and unroll. Dust your hands with sifted icing sugar and with your palms smooth the fondant over the surface, gently easing it to cover the cake.

Should any small air bubbles appear under the icing, prick them with a pin, then lightly rub the spot with your finger, or the heel of your hand.

Lift the cake onto a covered board and trim the surplus fondant away from the base with a broad-bladed sharp knife.

If using pincers or crimpers to decorate the edge of the cake, mark this edging while the fondant is still soft.

Wait until the icing has set before decorating the cake.

During hot, humid weather there is often a

Preparing the cake for the final covering: after the almond paste has set, brush the surface with un-beaten egg white before adding the fondant coat.

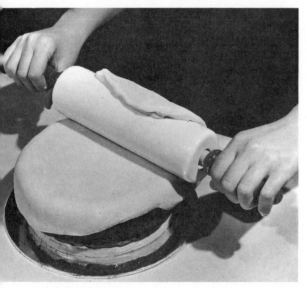

Covering the cake with fondant: roll the fondant a little smaller than the overall surface measure-ment and lift onto the cake with the aid of a rolling-pin.

tendency for fondant icing to become soft and sticky. To overcome this, buy some silica-gel crystals and place them in the container with the covered cake. The crystals absorb the moisture in the atmosphere and keep the cake dry. As they absorb it, they change to a green colour. To dry out the crystals for re-use, place them in the warm oven after you have been baking: they dry out gradually as it cools down.

Modelling Paste

For modelling some flowers, particularly those with larger petals, it is sometimes advisable to use a modelling paste in preference to fondant.

> 1 teaspoon copha or white vegetable shortening
> 1 slightly rounded teaspoon gelatine
> $1\frac{1}{2}$ tablespoons water
> $\frac{3}{4}$ lb. sifted icing sugar

Combine the copha, gelatine and water in a small saucepan and stir over low heat until the copha has melted and the gelatine has dissolved.

Sift $\frac{1}{2}$ lb. of the icing sugar into a bowl. Make a well in the centre and add the cooled but not set copha mixture.

Stir with a wooden spoon, gradually working in the dry icing sugar. The mixture at this stage will be soft. Turn it onto a board on which the remaining $\frac{1}{4}$ lb. of sifted icing sugar has been thickly spread, and knead, gradually working in the extra icing sugar until you have a good consistency for modelling.

To tint this paste add a few drops of vegetable colouring and knead the dough until the colour is evenly blended.

This type of paste does not require flavouring. Keep it in a covered container when not in use.

The Use of Food Colourings in Icings

It is most important that the only colourings used for tinting icing should be edible vegetable colourings. These are available in either powder or liquid form. Of the two the liquid is the most popular, but there may be occasions when you want, say, a strong red, and then it is more satisfactory to use both red powder and red liquid, so as to get the desired shade without upsetting the consistency or balance of the royal icing or the covering or modelling fondant.

All reliable brands of vegetable colourings are rather strong, and since most cakes are tinted rather than coloured only a very small amount of colouring should be used.

With royal icing the colour is added after the icing has been made. Drop a little from the end of a skewer and beat it in, making sure that it is evenly distributed before adding any more. Never pour it from the bottle: remember that you can always add more colouring, but you can't take it out once it has been mixed with the icing.

With fondant icing, if you know you will want only the one shade, the vegetable colouring may be added with the egg white, but if you intend using some of the fondant in a different shade, add the colouring after the icing has been made: it will be distributed evenly if it is kneaded into the fondant.

There will be times when either moulded or piped flowers and leaves are required in a deeper shade than that obtained by adding the colouring to the icing. In this case, mould or pipe the flowers or leaves in white, then, when they are dry, apply the pure, undiluted colouring, using a small watercolour brush.

You will need each of the primary colours— red, yellow and blue— and from these you will be able to produce quite a range of other colours. The rules an artist follows in mixing his colours apply as well here: the proper proportion of blue with yellow will give green; red and blue will produce violet, and so on.

Study the accompanying wheel for other colours.

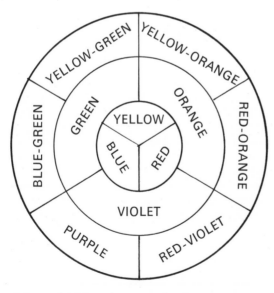

Colour wheel for use as a guide when mixing icing colours

Pipework

With any type of handwork, skill is developed only with constant practice. In cake decorating the first step is to become familiar with the various icing tubes. Begin with the writing tube, than try the leaf, the basket-weave, and the different sizes of star tubes. Don't attempt any work with the petal tube until you are thoroughly experienced in line and border work.

As you will be doing a lot of practice before you start on the cake itself you'll need something firm to work on: an upturned cake tin is good for this, or a sheet of thick glass. As you work, the icing can be scraped off, returned to the bowl, beaten up, and replaced in the bag for further practice.

The sheet of thick glass is a good idea: it not only gives you a firm working surface but as you become more proficient with the icing tubes you can place a simple design or border pattern under the glass and reproduce it on top.

Always use royal icing for practice. Place the tube in the bag if you are working with a paper cone; attach it to the screw if using a waterproof bag. Place your hand round the bag, turn the top back and spoon the icing in. Avoid having too much in the bag at the one time, for a very full bag is difficult to handle.

If using an icing bag made of paper, fold the top over the icing to seal it in. To do this hold the bag in the palm of the left hand; when the icing has been spooned in, press the front of the bag with the thumb to cover the icing, then bring the top of the bag down over the part just held by the thumb. Make several folds for a complete seal.

If a waterproof bag is being used, hold it loosely in the left hand with the tube hanging down. Turn the top of the bag back over your fingers. Spoon in the icing, turn the top back again, then twist it at the level of the icing. Grasp the bag with your working hand, holding the twisted section between the first finger and thumb: this pressure at the top of the bag prevents the icing from oozing out.

Holding the bag in your right hand, guide it lightly with the tip of the forefinger of your left hand. The pressure from the fingers of the right hand forces the icing out of the bag in an even flow.

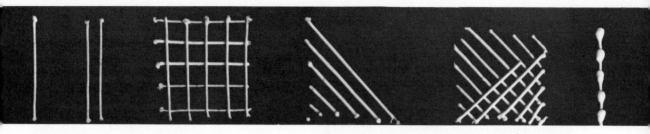

THE WRITING TUBE

Many of the designs in this book call for the use of the writing tube. Until you are experienced, work with a number 1 tube: a finer tube will make the work more difficult for a beginner.

Practise making vertical and parallel lines, then cross the lines to form an evenly spaced lattice pattern. Hold the icing tube upright with its point lightly touching the surface of the cake at the place where you want to start piping a design. Squeeze the bag lightly, at the same time lifting the tube from the cake. Continuing to squeeze the icing through the tube at an even pressure, slowly and carefully draw the thread of icing in a straight line for the required distance. Cease the pressure on the bag and gently lower the tube until it lightly touches the cake again. Lift it quickly so that the thread of icing will break off where it has just touched the cake.

If the tube is allowed to touch the cake while the thread is being drawn across the surface, the resulting line will be crooked or misshapen.

Now try some dots with the same icing tube. This may sound easy, but it takes a little practice to obtain a good rounded surface. Place the point of the tube on the cake's surface and squeeze the bag lightly, keeping the tube upright. Squeeze, stop, and lift the tube from the cake. You may find that at first you are drawing the icing up into a point instead of leaving it in a rounded dot. The proper effect will come with practice, but you can help mould the dot into shape with the moistened tip of a fine water-colour brush.

Use this method to make the five tiny petals of a forget-me-not. Incidentally, this flower may be piped either directly onto the cake or onto waxed paper—in the latter case allow the flower to dry before attaching it with a tiny dot of icing. When a forget-me-not is piped on paper it is most important to make each of the five dots touch, otherwise the flower will break when being lifted from the paper.

Simple designs for practice with a writing tube

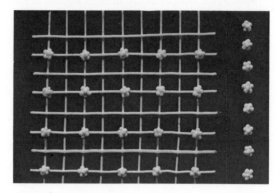

Lattice and forget-me-nots done with a writing tube

BASKET WEAVE

This type of decoration is applied directly to the cake. There are three versions. One, as shown here, is done with the basket-weave tube alone; the second, shown in the Basket of Roses Cake on page 57, is made with a writing tube and a basket-weave tube; the third, sometimes referred to as wicker-work, seen in the Pram Cake on page 89, uses the same method but is done with a writing tube only.

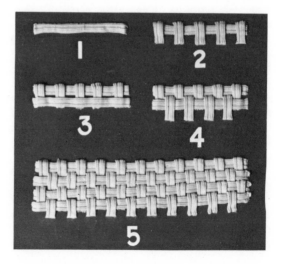

Always commence basket-weave at the top of the cake. Guide lines may be marked with a pin or a fine skewer; use a ruler to make sure they are straight. Have the royal icing well worked, and a little stiffer than for lattice work. Hold the bag with the edge of the tube flat on the cake but barely touching, and squeeze the icing out to make a horizontal line level with the edge of the cake.

Now make short vertical lines at regular intervals over the first line. Follow with another horizontal line, making sure that a line of icing covers both ends of the short vertical lines.

The second row of vertical lines is placed midway between those in the line above it, giving the desired interlaced effect.

When both the writing tube and the basket-weave tube are used for this work (as in the Basket of Roses Cake), pipe the horizontal lines with the basket-weave tube and the vertical lines with the writing tube. For the wicker work, use the writing tube for all lines.

THE STAR TUBE

This is possibly one of the easiest tubes to use, and a number of designs can be made with it, as the illustration shows. Stars and dots are made with this tube in the same way as described for the writing tube, but they cannot be touched up with a brush.

Use royal or butter icing of a firm consistency so that it will keep its shape when piped. Hold the icing bag upright and have the tip of the tube lightly touching the cake. Squeeze the bag, applying only enough pressure to produce the size star required. Cease the pressure, then quickly lift the tube from the cake.

Shell edging, a popular trimming for the base of a cake, is made with the star tube. Hold the bag in a slightly slanting position and apply pressure only long enough to produce a rounded shape. Now gently draw the point of the tube away very slightly and, without lifting it from the cake, apply more pressure to make a shell that just overlaps the point of the first shell shape.

A double shell edge is made with the same action, but the shells are zigzagged instead of being piped in a straight line.

The curlicue, or reverse shell, is similar to the plain shell, but as each shell is built up, circle the tube to the right as the pressure is eased: follow

this with a circle to the left, lifting the tube between each shell and reversing the circle as you pipe another shell.

The rope design is generally used for the lower border of a large cake. As it is rather a heavy type of decoration, use a finer tube—number 5 Australian or the corresponding one in the English range (see page 4). Hold the icing bag at an angle of about 45 degrees, with the tube lightly touching the cake. Squeeze the icing out with an even pressure, lifting it from the cake as it emerges from the tube and gently twisting it into a loop. Steady, even pressure and a straight eye combine to make a success of this border design.

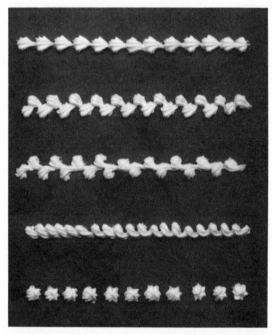

Designs made with a star tube: shell, double shell, curlicue, rope, and stars

THE LEAF TUBE

There will be times when the leaf tube may be used for a border or a ruffle, but it is mainly intended for making leaves to trim flower or fruit sprays.

To have a well-defined vein down the centre of the piped leaf the icing must be of a good consistency: if it is too soft it will merely produce a shapeless blob instead of a leaf.

Hold the icing bag in a slightly slanting position and allow the tip of the tube to touch the surface of the cake very lightly. Squeeze the bag gently: the icing will fan out of the notched tube. Let it frill slightly by holding the bag still and applying a little pressure, then gradually ease off the pressure before lifting the tube from the cake. As the tube is gently drawn away, the icing will taper to a point.

If the point of a leaf is not as well defined as it should be you can fix it by pinching the tip of the leaf shape lightly with the first finger and thumb.

When you want two-toned leaves place alternate spoonfuls of reddish-brown and green icing in the same bag. As the icing is squeezed through the tube the colours combine to give an attractive variegated effect.

Leaves and ruffle (top), leaves with stem and tendrils (lower left), and leaves and grapes, all made with a leaf tube

HOLDING A PAPER ICING BAG

When a paper icing bag is used, the pressure is applied with the thumb and fingers. This method is most suited to light lace-work or outline work.

Net Appliqué Work

This is particularly suitable for wedding and christening cakes. It is best done on the finer bridal tulle—sometimes the coarser tulle tends to crack or break the icing when the motif is being attached to the cake.

If you haven't a piece of lace, say from the bride's dress, that you would like to copy, then use a needlework transfer.

Place the design on a flat board and cover it with tulle. Pin the corners to keep the net firmly in position. Outline the design, using a well-worked royal icing through a fine tube, or through a paper icing bag with a fine opening.

Leave until the icing is almost dry, then, using either sharp-pointed scissors or a razor blade, trim away the tulle, leaving the lace motif intact.

If you wish to give the lace motif (perhaps it is a net appliqué leaf) a curved or rounded shape, place it over a shaped surface such as the back of a wooden spoon or the handle of the rolling-pin and allow it to set.

Attach this type of decoration to the cake with pinpoints of royal icing.

Net appliqué: outline with royal icing and cut out the shape when it is almost dry.

The Cake Border

STRING BORDERS

String work is done with a fine writing tube and is most suitable for the side decoration on a cake.

Royal icing is used, and care should be taken to see that it has been well worked and is of the correct consistency: if it is too thin or soft it will not hold together, nor will it remain on the side of the cake when piped. If it is too stiff it will not "string out" or flow smoothly.

For practice it is a good idea to use the side of a cake tin. Turn the cake tin upside down and use the edge as a guide line. Touch the tin with the tip of the tube and begin squeezing with an even pressure.

On no account move your hand up and down: let the gravity pull the icing string down.

For the small string scallop or drop (see illustration), as the icing issues from the tube move it along and touch or anchor it every quarter of an inch, pressing or squeezing just enough to enable the line of icing to fall to a depth of a quarter of an inch. Your piping hand should be at the top of the tin all the time: if you allow it to follow the dropped line of icing you will find it impossible to obtain even or regular sized loops or scallops.

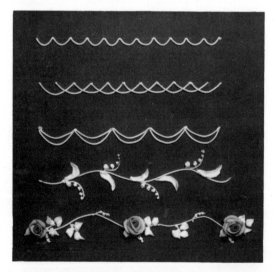

String borders: small string scallop, double string scallop, deeper scallop, lily-of-the-valley border, and rose border

For the double string scallop work in the same way as for the single but touch the cake at half-inch intervals and commence each succeeding scallop at the centre of the previous one.

For a deeper single scallop mark the cake at one-inch intervals with a pin. Use the pin marks as your guide line and commence by placing the tip of the tube on one of them. Squeeze the icing out with steady pressure, letting the thread fall to a depth of about half an inch before moving on to touch the next pin mark. When these single scallops have been applied all round the cake, go round again with a second row of single scallops, this time allowing the line to drop about a quarter of an inch below the first.

For the lily-of-the-valley border a single free-flowing curved line is piped, using a number 1 writing tube. The long narrow leaves are made with the smallest leaf tube, or use a cone of paper with its tip cut to the shape of a leaf. The leaves of lily-of-the-valley should be piped from the inside of each curve of the stem. The small white bell-shaped flowers are piped on the stems with a number 1 writing tube.

Rose borders, suitable for wedding or birthday cakes, require either moulded or piped flowers already prepared. A fine writing tube is used to make the curved stems and also the tendrils, which are placed between the flowers and the leaves. A leaf tube makes the foliage. When the leaves, stems and tendrils have been piped onto the cake, attach each rose with a dab of royal icing.

Two more variations, which are self-explanatory, are shown. The first one is made with a single shell shape that is repeated: it gives the impression of a flower when the three slightly curved lines are overpiped at the base, and it is completed with a vandyke pattern piped with a fine writing tube. The second is a variation of the string border: to make the scallops even, first pipe dots with a number 1 tube at regular intervals round the cake, then in piping the scallops bring the tube to every alternate dot.

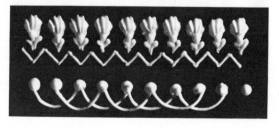

ANOTHER ATTRACTIVE BORDER

A simple and effective border design is made with a fine and a coarser writing tube.

First make a row of dots with a number 2 writing tube, making sure they are evenly spaced. Above each dot, and using the same tube, make smaller dots with tips, each tip pointing to the top of the cake. Leave until dry.

Now change to a number 0 writing tube and run a wavy line across the larger dot. Then over the smaller dot, pipe three short lines, the centre one following the shape of the top dot, and the two side ones curling to the right and the left.

This design is seen on the accompanying wedding cake picture.

An attractive light border design made with a fine and a coarser writing tube

The light border design is shown here on a two-tier cake.

Butterflies

Using royal icing on waxed paper it is possible to make either flooded or filigree butterflies.

MAKING A FLOODED BUTTERFLY

The wings are made in the same way as for a flooded key (page 61); first outline them on waxed paper, then fill in the outlines with softened royal icing. The body of the butterfly is piped directly onto the cake, then, as the icing dries, the wings are placed in position. To support the wings at an angle, put a small ball of cotton wool underneath each one. Remove the cotton wool as the icing dries.

The antennae are attached while the icing is still soft. Flower stamens are useful for butterfly antennae, but if these are not available, pipe thin lines on waxed paper, allow to dry, then attach to the butterfly's head by means of tweezers.

FILIGREE BUTTERFLY ON NET

To make one of these butterflies you will first need to draw or trace the outline on a piece of paper, cover with waxed paper and then with a piece of net. Now follow the picture guide and instructions.

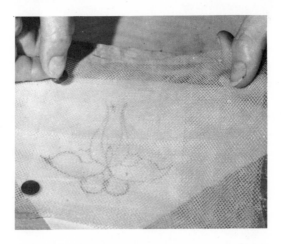

Making a net butterfly. Step 1: Trace or draw the outline on a piece of paper, cover with waxed paper and then with a piece of fine net; pin securely to a board.

Step 2: With well-worked royal icing and a fine writing tube outline the design on the net, using a slightly damp fine brush to ease the icing into the curves; fill in the outline with fine dots or lattice; leave to set till the following day.

Step 3: Lift the net carefully from the paper and with a small pair of scissors trim the surplus away, leaving the butterfly reinforced with net; for double strength, turn the butterfly over and outline the shape on the wrong side with icing.

Step 4: To attach to the cake, run a little royal icing down the butterfly's body on the wrong side; holding the motif by the wing tips, lightly press to the corners of the cake; allow to dry thoroughly before handling again.

Piped Flowers

Making your own flowers, tinting them to the desired colour and having them the appropriate size and shape means that you can produce a really individually designed cake.

The icing, which should be a well-worked royal mixture, should be beaten to the stage when a little, lifted from the wooden spoon, will stand in strong peaks. The addition of a few drops of acetic acid will help make the flowers firmer when piped.

With the exception of forget-me-nots and wisteria, most flowers cannot be piped directly onto the cake. Instead, they are built up petal by petal, either round a wooden toothpick or the tapered end of a fine watercolour brush or on a piece of waxed paper about one inch square. For this work, an icing petal tube is required.

When hand-made flowers are to form the main decoration on a cake, it is recommended that an adequate supply be made from the same quantity of icing: this will ensure that they are all the same colour and have petals of the same texture.

A few simple icing tools are all you need to make piped sugar flowers: they include icing nails, writing and petal tubes, and paper icing bags. The pincers may be used to make an edging.

ROSES

These are possibly the most popular of all the piped flowers for cake decorating. For all piped flowers see that a well-worked royal icing of a firm but not dry consistency is in readiness: if it is too slack the roses will not hold their shape and if it is too dry the edges of the petals will break as they are piped.

One colour alone may be used, or the centres may be piped in a deeper colour than the outside petals. If you want the two tones you'll need only the one icing bag: the bud or centre of the flower is made in the deeper shade and left to dry, then the lighter coloured outside petals are added.

The first step is to pipe the bud shape that forms the centre. This is done by holding the wooden toothpick on which the rose is to be piped in the left hand. Now, with the bag in the right hand, and the point of the tube pointing down, circle the tip of the pick twice as you squeeze the icing out.

Now make three petals round each centre. To do this, hold the wooden toothpick in the same position, and, beginning at the base, pipe a half-circle. Turn the pick slightly and repeat the action, overlapping the commencement of the first petal as the stick is turned. Repeat once more, forming the third petal.

For the final row of piping, make five petals, each one a half-circle and each one slightly overlapping the edge of the previous petal.

When piping these petals try to keep the wooden pick in the same upright position, turning it as you pipe each petal.

There are two ways of handling the piped roses. If they are piped on toothpicks they may be placed in the pick board (see illustration on page 4) and left until almost dry, then carefully lifted off onto waxed paper to become completely dry. Or they can be taken off the tapered end of the watercolour brush with the aid of a piece of cardboard which has slits about a quarter of an inch in depth cut in the edges. Each rose is removed as soon as it has been piped and allowed to dry on the cardboard. Either method is satisfactory.

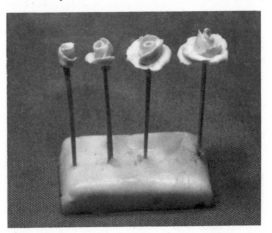

Piped roses

Tiny piped roses make an effective border for this wedding anniversary cake; leaves and fine tendrils complete the side design.

17

PANSIES

These are piped directly onto small squares of waxed paper. Attach the paper to either an icing nail or the end of a wooden spoon, using a small dab of icing.

You need a medium-size petal tube and well-worked royal icing. Holding the petal tube with its wide or thick end pointing down, make the first petal, using an "outward and return" movement. Turn the paper slightly and pipe the second petal with the same movement, but slightly overlapping the first.

Now pipe the third petal, which will slightly overlap the first petal on the left. The fourth petal, which will match the third, is on the opposite side of the flower; revolve the paper and pipe this petal, overlapping the first petal slightly.

For the fifth and final petal which is the base petal and the largest, turn the piped flower so that the first two petals are facing downwards. Using a wider sweep of icing, pipe in this large base petal so that it overlaps the bottom edges of the third and fourth petals.

When the petals are dry, pipe a spot of contrasting icing in the centre, using a writing tube, and for a more realistic effect touch up the inner section of each petal with pure vegetable colouring, applying it with a brush.

SWEET PEAS

One of the simplest flowers to pipe is the sweet pea. This is piped onto waxed paper and allowed to dry before removing.

Using a petal tube and fairly stiff royal icing, hold the bag almost parallel to the paper. With the long end of the tube downwards, pipe a three-quarter circle or horseshoe shape. Slightly uneven pressure on the bag will give a ruffled edge to the petals.

Repeat the same movement, but this time pipe the icing inside the horseshoe shape.

Now add the centre simply by squeezing the icing in an up-and-down movement, holding the tube upright.

Allow to dry before adding the green calyx with a writing tube.

Sweet pea buds. These can be very useful in sprays, or for the decoration on the sides of a cake. They are easy to make and may be piped directly onto the cake. Follow the directions for making the sweet pea flowers, but pipe only the three-quarter circle and the centre.

JONQUILS

These are made up of two sets of three petals with a cone shape for the centre.

Have yellow-tinted royal icing for the petals and a white cone centre. Or have white petals with a yellow centre.

Using the petal tube, pipe three evenly spaced petals onto greased paper. Allow them to partly dry, then fill in the spaces with the second set of three petals.

Before the petals are quite dry add the centre cone, using a fine writing tube and building up the round you have made in the centre until it forms a cup or cone.

If the centres are white they can be touched up when dry with a deeper coloured yellow icing.

WISTERIA

This is one of the flowers which may be piped either onto waxed paper or directly onto the cake. Use a good stiff royal icing and a petal tube.

Begin at the tip of the flower head and, holding the icing bag upright, pipe the first petal. The movement is an up-and-down stroking action, and no one petal should be more than a quarter of an inch in length.

On either side of the first petal, commencing half-way down the petal, pipe another. Lift the tube after each.

For the third row add three petals, one on each side of the first upright petal and the third down the centre.

Each row should slightly overlap the previous one.

Continue in rows, increasing the number of petals. It is usual to have four or five petals in the final row, but this could vary according to the size flower required.

Add the green calyx after the flower petals have dried.

Allow the flowers to dry completely before attempting to remove them from the paper.

With practice you can make a variety of flower shapes. Here you see roses, jonquils, carnations, sweet peas, apple blossom, and wisteria. All were piped with royal icing through a petal tube. Shown in colour on page 103.

APPLE BLOSSOM

Use any of the petal tubes, the smaller one for tiny blossoms. Hold the tube at an angle of about 45 degrees, lightly touching the waxed paper which has been pinned to a firm board, and make the first petals in a half circular movement, varying the pressure if you want a frilly edge.

Keep the long or pointed end of the tube in the centre of the flower. Five petals usually make up this blossom.

Allow the flower to dry, then with a contrasting colour pipe small dots in the centre of each flower.

19

CARNATIONS

For the best effect with this flower you will want a fairly stiff icing.

Place a small square of waxed paper on the flat surface of an icing nail. Using a petal tube, and with the long or pointed end lightly touching the paper, make a circle of five frilly petals, all touching in the centre.

Inside this circle make three more petals, this time raising them slightly so that they will fill the centre of the flower.

Two colours in the one icing bag gives a better effect for this flower.

Half carnations. These are useful for the side decoration on cakes. Hold the long end of the icing tube against the paper on the icing nail and make three or four frilly petals, each one overlapping the previous petal. Holding the tube almost at right angles to the flower, pipe three more petals slightly below the first four. Allow to dry before adding the green calyx with a number 2 writing tube.

DAISIES

These flowers are best piped on a small square of paper attached to the flat surface of an icing nail with a small dab of royal icing.

Before you begin piping place a small dot in the centre. This will help to keep your petals centred.

Using short stroking movements put the first petal in an upright position. Slowly turn the nail as the remaining petals are piped.

The last petal will be the most difficult. If it is not quite uniform it may be adjusted with the aid of your fine dry watercolour brush.

Add a dab of coloured icing for the centre.

Moulded Flowers

Two types of icing are used for moulding flowers for decorating a cake. One is the fondant (recipe on page 6), the same as is used for covering the cake, and the other is a modelling paste (recipe on page 9). It is a matter of personal choice which one is used, and unless you are making flowers with large petals, such as gladioli or orchids, the fondant is perfectly satisfactory.

Make up the fondant in white, then add the colour a few drops at a time, kneading it in until it has been well blended.

ROSES

Colour the paste for pastel roses. Take a small piece and, with the fingers dipped in either sifted icing sugar or cornflour, work it until it is paper thin. For a small rose it should measure about half an inch wide and three-quarters to one inch long. Roll it up to form the centre of the rose.

Take another piece, work it up, then divide it into two and make two petals. Fit them on either side of the centre. They should overlap.

Using the same shaping for the petals, make three or four more and overlap them round the last two you have placed in position.

With scissors cut away the surplus from the back of the rose and place the flower on waxed paper to dry.

For two-toned roses make the centre from a deeper coloured fondant than the outer petals.

FRANGIPANI

These are made from five uniformly shaped petals moulded in white fondant or paste, the yellow colour being applied after the flowers have dried.

Instead of modelling the petals, roll the fondant thinly and cut it into half-inch rounds with a cutter. Pull each round to make it into a slight oval, then pinch one end of the petal to give it the correct shape.

Assemble the five petals, each one slightly overlapping the one before it, to give a slightly conical flower.

Leave until dry, then paint the centre with yellow vegetable colouring.

JONQUILS

These are made up of two sets of white or yellow petals slightly pointed at the ends, and with a faint ridge down the centre.

Mould the six petals and place them in position as shown, then, using the tapered end of a water-colour brush, press the ends of the petals together in the centre.

Colour some of the paste a bright yellow and form small cups for the centre. The end of a pencil will make a cup shape.

Attach the cups to the centre of the flowers with a dab of royal icing.

SINGLE BLOSSOMS

These may be moulded from fondant or from the modelling paste. Because the petals are larger you may have more success with the paste rather than the fondant.

The stamens are those used in French-flower making. They are not piped.

Take small pieces of the paste and mould it with the fingers to make slightly hollow petals. You will need five for each flower. Place a tiny ball of the paste on a waxed paper sheet and

Moulded roses and lilies form an attractive decoration on this two-tier wedding cake; the leaves and stems are piped.

moisten it lightly with water or egg white.

Arrange the petals overlapping one another to form the flower. The points of the petals should be touching the small ball of paste. Press them down lightly and leave the flower to dry. If the paste or fondant you are using is the correct consistency the flower will hold its shape.

When dry, attach the centre of artificial stamens, using a dab of royal icing.

LILIES

These are the easiest of all the flowers to mould. Dust a pastry board with either sifted icing sugar or cornflour and roll the fondant or modelling paste thinly. Cut it into one-inch squares. Using some of the scraps, work a little colouring into them to make a yellow mixture.

21

Form the yellow fondant into thin rolls about the thickness of a match. Place one diagonally on each square, then roll up into a cone shape.

Press the pointed end of each cone to anchor the spike, and trim off any excess with the scissors.

PANSIES

If you wish to make life-size pansies use modelling paste rather than fondant. It holds better.

Shape five petals from pastel yellow or mauve paste, the lower front petal to be a little larger than the others.

Assemble them on a small ball of moistened paste and leave until dry.

With a fine watercolour brush apply the desired tonings and shadings to the flowers, using food colourings.

VIOLAS

Five petals make up this little flower, which may be moulded from coloured fondant or paste, or moulded in white and coloured after it has dried.

Place the two top petals in position first, lapping the right one over the left, then add the two side petals so that they slightly overlap the top petals. Make the lower front petal slightly larger than the other four and place it so that it overlaps part of the side petals (the illustration will help to make this clear).

When dry, touch up the colours with a fine brush.

SWEET PEAS

The sweet pea consists of three pieces and is a very easily moulded flower.

Take a piece of modelling paste or fondant and make a fairly large, flat petal with a slightly fluted edge for the back. Now make a similar one a shade smaller in size and place it over the first one. A light brushing of unbeaten egg white or water will keep it in position.

Take a thinner piece of paste, mould into much the same shape as the first two then fold it lightly in two. This is placed in the centre of the second petal.

Use a little green royal icing through a fine writing tube for the green calyx at the base of each flower.

SINGLE AZALEAS

Artificial stamens such as those used for French flowers and sometimes referred to as milliner's stamens are necessary for these flowers.

Roll the fondant icing a little more than an eighth of an inch in thickness. Cut into lengths about an inch long. Using a small sharp-pointed knife make four slits, each about a quarter of an inch in depth, in one edge of the icing. Now twist the icing into a round. Run the tapered end of the handle of a watercolour brush down the centre to make a tubular flower, then, with the fingers dusted in sifted icing sugar, flatten each petal. Pinch the end of each into a peak. Cut off about half a dozen artificial stamens and attach them to the inside of the flower with a little royal icing.

HYACINTHS

These are made in the same way, but the paste is cut into five instead of four, which will give six petals for each hyacinth. Stamens are not used in these flowers, but for a more realistic effect press the side of the brush into the flattened petal to give the impression of the deeper core in each hyacinth flower, and bring the points to a more definite peak.

Clipper Work

Clipper work, which is done while the covering fondant icing is still soft, can provide a simple, quick, and effective border on a cake. It may be used as the sole decoration on the sides of the cake, or as a basis for more elaborate pipework.

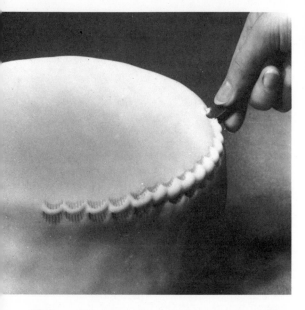

Clipper work: before the icing sets, pinch an edge round the cake with the special clippers.

A little practice is essential to ascertain how much pressure is necessary. The idea is to hold the clippers or pincers open with the serrated ends about a quarter of an inch apart, press them lightly into the icing where you want the design, then apply a little firmer pressure until they are about an eighth of an inch apart.

Before you lift the clippers from the cake, release the pressure to allow the serrated ends to reopen to the original quarter inch. Unless you do this there is a risk of lifting and pulling away the pressed section of the icing.

These clippers, which are made of metal, come in various shapes and sizes and are usually available from stores or shops that sell cake decorating equipment.

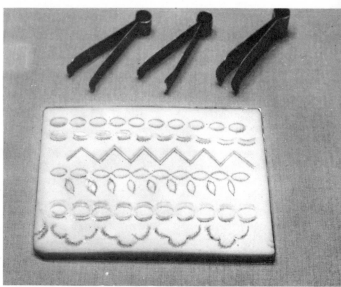

The clippers, made of metal, come in various shapes and sizes. Here are some examples of what can be done with them.

Almond Artistry

One fascinating branch of cake decorating is modelling in almond paste. Once you have mastered the art there's no limit to the number of shapes and designs you can use to give variety to your cakes.

23

All the shapes illustrated in the following pages have been made from ready-to-use almond paste bought by the packet. The paste is coloured with the same food colourings as are used for icing and confectionery.

No expensive tools or elaborate equipment are necessary for modelling this paste: you rely on ordinary household knives, pastry cutters, scissors and a rolling-pin. For a fancy surface simply wind some plastic-covered electric flex around an ordinary rolling-pin. The effect is seen in Santa's beard or in the duck's beak (this page and page 25). The cutters used for the bird's beak are ordinary round pastry cutters: the beak is pushed into shape after cutting.

The chocolate used for dipping the almond shapes is a cooking chocolate.

A little sifted icing sugar should be dusted on the hands and on the board when working the almond paste. Colours are kneaded into the paste before it is shaped.

Almond paste is soft and pliable and there should not be any difficulty in shaping it; but once it dries, the shapes cannot be altered.

SANTA

Using some red coloured almond paste make a thin round strip about 10 inches long. Twist as shown in the picture, then snip the curve at the bottom to form the two legs.

Roll a piece of pink and red paste with a flex-covered rolling-pin and cut with an oval cutter. The red tip forms the cap and the pink the face. Mark in the eyes with white icing and chocolate, the nose with red paste and the mouth with yellow paste.

A piece of white paste may be used for the moustache, or the beard and the moustache may be applied with some royal icing on a brush.

RUDOLF THE REINDEER

Roll two pieces of chocolate almond paste into sticks about 3 inches long and ½ inch thick.

Cut one piece in half and shape the head. Pull up the antlers from the other cut half, and snip below them for the ears. Point the nose.

Use the other long piece of paste for the body, slitting both ends with a knife to form the legs. Now curve the shape into a half-circle and snip one end of the tail. Cross the back legs and allow the paste to dry.

When both pieces are quite dry and firm, dip

the undersides only in chocolate, covering the two front and one rear foot with the chocolate.

Attach the head to the body. Make the eyes of white icing and chocolate and apply a dab of red colouring for the tip of the nose.

A piece of paste, coloured red and cut into a circle, forms the saddle.

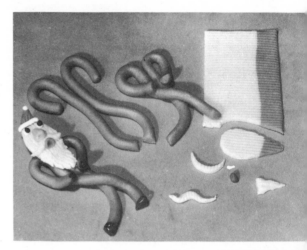

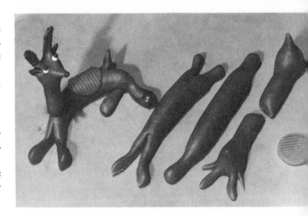

SAMMY THE SEAL

One long piece of uncoloured almond paste about 2½ inches long and a little more than ½ inch thick makes the seal.

Narrow the paste at both ends, form one into a point for the head, and slit the other end with a knife for the tail.

About two-thirds down the body snip on either side with a knife to make the flippers. Turn the paste so that the seal lies flat on the table. Raise the head and support it with a rolling-pin until it becomes firm and dry.

24

Dip completely in chocolate. Allow to dry, then add eyes of white icing and chocolate.

For the ball you will need both red and uncoloured almond icing. Make two separate rolls, each about ½ inch thick. Cut each one into four and join the red pieces and the uncoloured pieces alternately. Roll between the hands to make smooth, then cut into ½-inch slices. Roll one of these slices into a ball in the hand and attach to the nose of the seal with a little chocolate.

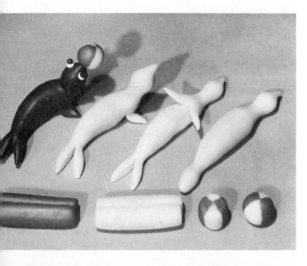

DAFFY THE DUCK

Make a ball of plain almond paste about one inch in diameter, then shape it into an oval.

Make a ½-inch ball for the head. On the larger ball of paste pull up a point for the tail, then mark the wings with the back of a knife.

From some rolled yellow-coloured paste cut out a shape one inch long for the bill. Shape it so

that it is about one-third of an inch wide at the end and about ¼ inch wide in the centre. Attach this to the head of the duck with the aid of a wooden skewer.

Join the head to the body with chocolate, and use white icing and chocolate for the eyes.

Complete the duck by dipping the base in melted chocolate.

PERCY THE PENGUIN

Take a piece of uncoloured almond paste approximately one inch thick and 2½ inches long. Mould into a pear shape. Point up the end to form the penguin's beak and, while it is still soft, pull the beak to the front.

With a small sharp-pointed knife snip the paste below the neck and open out to form the flippers.

Now melt some chocolate over hot, not boiling, water and, using an icing bag made of paper, pipe a V on a piece of waxed paper, for the feet. Allow to become set and dry.

Dip the body of the penguin in chocolate, submerging all but the beak and front. Allow to dry.

Use a little softened chocolate to attach the feet, standing the penguin upright. (For a firmer shape, dip the feet in more chocolate before attaching to the body.) Use white icing and chocolate for the eyes.

OSCAR THE OWL

Begin with a piece of green-coloured almond paste 2 inches long, one inch wide, and about ½ inch thick.

Pinch the paste at one end to form the ears, then narrow it slightly for the neck. Place on the table and roll lightly with a flex-covered rolling-pin.

Using a small sharp-pointed knife snip about half-way down the sides for the wings. Ease these so that they stand out, then, using a pair of scissors, snip the centre of the head for the beak.

Make the feet by piping some softened chocolate through a paper cone into a V shape on waxed paper. When set and dry, attach to the body, standing the owl upright.

Dabs of white icing and beads of chocolate make the eyes.

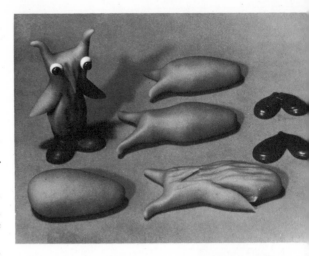

BUSTER THE BUNNY

Make a ball of brown almond paste about 1½ inches in diameter for the body, and an oval shape 1½ inches long and ¾ inch thick for the head.

Pinch the body piece with scissors to form the tail. Pull up one end of the oval piece to form the ears, and mould these with the fingers to make them smooth.

When both pieces of paste have become set, attach the head to the body with softened chocolate and then dip the whole shape in chocolate, covering the base and the narrow end of the body.

Mark a cross in chocolate for the mouth, and use white icing and beads of chocolate for the eyes.

KITTY THE CAT

Take two pieces of orange-coloured almond paste and mould one into a ball about 1½ inches in diameter and the other into a ball ¾ inch in diameter.

Flatten the large ball slightly, then, using a round cutter about the same size as the ball, cut half-way round, to make a tail about ¼ inch in diameter. Carefully twist this cut piece to form a curled tail.

Pinch up ears on the smaller ball of paste, and, when set, attach this ball, the head, to the body with a little softened chocolate.

Allow the shape to become set and dry, then dip the base in softened chocolate. Mark the nose with a dab of chocolate, and use white icing and a dab or bead of chocolate for the eyes.

CHARLIE THE CHICKEN

Take a piece of yellow almond paste and roll it into a ball about one inch in diameter. Now flatten it slightly and make two slits with a sharp knife about half-way through the paste about $\frac{1}{2}$ inch apart. This forms the body of the chicken. Make another ball of the same coloured paste about $\frac{1}{2}$ inch in diameter for the head.

Dip the base of the body in chocolate, allowing it to come about $\frac{1}{4}$ inch up the sides. Attach the head to the body with a dab of chocolate, and make the eyes from white icing and a bead of chocolate.

Colour a little of the paste red and roll it thinly, using a flex-covered rolling-pin. Cut a $\frac{1}{2}$-inch diamond shape from this rolled paste and, with the point of a wooden skewer, press it into the centre of the head to make an open beak.

A little red royal icing is piped on top for the comb.

Log Cabin Cake

You will need:
A rich fruit cake, butter weight $\frac{1}{2}$ lb., baked in a $7\frac{1}{2}$-inch square cake tin (recipe on page 133)
1 lb. almond paste
Apricot jam for glazing
One quantity of royal icing
2 packets chocolate finger biscuits
2 chocolates for tree tubs

Food colourings
A wisp of cotton wool
Wooden toothpicks

Bake the cake at 275°F. for $3\frac{1}{2}$ to 4 hours. Leave for several days before decorating.

Cut a $2\frac{1}{2}$-inch-wide piece from one side of the cake. Cut this piece diagonally from top right-hand edge to bottom left-hand edge. Lift the top half over the bottom half to the right and put the two halves together to form a triangular-shaped roof, joining them with a little thinned and sieved apricot jam.

Cut a one-inch strip from the remaining two-thirds of the cake, cut into three equal-sized pieces and place together (brushing each piece with the thinned apricot jam) to form the chimney.

If necessary trim the top of the large piece of cake so that the roof will sit evenly. Brush the surface with the thinned apricot jam and set the roof in position. Trim if necessary.

Colour the almond paste green by kneading into it a few drops of green colouring. Make the pattern as illustrated. Roll the almond paste thinly and cut two pieces from each pattern. Cut a door and windows from one of the larger pieces and a window from one of the smaller pieces.

Brush the surface of the cake with thinned and sieved apricot jam and press the almond paste into position. While still soft, mark the surface with the tines of a fork, or draw lines with the back of a knife, keeping them even with the aid of a ruler.

Cover the chimney with rolled almond paste and cut a V-shaped piece from the base where it will be attached to the roof. Set the chimney in position.

Using royal icing, attach the chocolate finger biscuits to form the roof, cutting the biscuits where necessary. Allow the biscuits to hang over the edge of the cake to form the eaves. Cut three biscuits for door panels and use a piece of almond paste for the door handle.

The trees. Mould two pieces of almond paste into cone shapes and press four toothpicks into the thick end of each to use as the base or trunk of the tree. Press the other end of the toothpicks into the chocolate tubs.

The "flagstones". Add some brown colouring to the left-over pieces of almond paste and knead only slightly to give a mottled effect. Roll thinly, cut into uneven shapes and fit together on a piece of board. Mount the cake on this paved board.

Roll tiny scraps of almond paste into tiny balls and brush them with orange colouring. These are for the fruit on the trees.

Colour some royal icing green, and using a small leaf tube, pipe leaves over the almond paste cone. When dry, attach the tiny pieces of fruit, using a dab of royal icing. Place the trees in front of the cabin. Add a wisp of cotton wool to the chimney for the smoke.

Chocolate biscuits make the roof and almond paste the walls of this novel log cabin cake. The tree tubs are also made of chocolate.
Shown in colour on page 103

Clown Cake

You will need:
 A light fruit or sultana cake, butter weight
 ½ lb., baked in an 8-inch cake tin (recipes
 on pages 32, 132)
 1½ to 2 lb. fondant icing
 Egg white for glazing
 A double quantity of royal icing
 Food colourings

Knead the white fondant icing and roll it out. Brush the surface of the cake lightly with unbeaten egg white and apply the icing.

Smooth with the hands, trim the base and leave for a day or two for the fondant to become firm.

Meanwhile, make the clowns. Trace the clown shape on waxed paper and outline it in white or yellow royal icing through a number 0 icing tube. Now flood in the figure, using blue and yellow icing which has been thinned down with either water or lemon juice. When the icing is quite dry, paint in the eyes, mouth and cap top.

Make the balls and the balloons in the same way. You will need five clowns, eight balls and three balloons.

When the flooded figures are dry, carefully remove them from the paper and attach them to the cake with a small dab of royal icing.

Pipe the strings to the balloons in black or brown icing and write the child's name on the centre balloon with a fine watercolour brush.

Use white icing through a star tube to make a shell border at the base.

The clown outline for flooding
Flood the ball in a colour of your choice.

Flooded figures of a clown and a ball trim this circus cake for a child's birthday.
Shown in colour on page 104

Any little girl would be thrilled with a pretty Dolly Varden cake for her birthday. The cake itself is a rich fruit mixture.
Shown in colour on page 104

Dolly Varden Cake

You couldn't have a more charming cake for a little girl's birthday than a Dolly Varden design. A rich fruit cake mixture is used, though if the child is very young a light fruit mixture is preferable.

At some stores you can buy a special Dolly Varden cake mould, but otherwise use a pudding basin large enough to hold ten cups of liquid (one of this size will accommodate the Dolly Varden cake mixture).

You will need:

> *A rich or a light fruit cake, butter weight*
> *½ lb., baked in a Dolly Varden cake mould*
> *or in a pudding basin (recipes on pages 132,*
> *133)*
> *½ lb. almond paste*
> *1 lb. fondant*
> *Egg white and apricot jam for glazing*
> *8 dozen two-tone roses*
> *Piped lace trim for panniers*
> *A doll top 4 in. high*
> *Lace, ribbon, and tulle*
> *One quantity of royal icing*
> *Food colourings*

Line the Dolly Varden mould or the pudding basin with one thickness of greaseproof paper. Place the mixture in this container and insulate the outside of it with two thicknesses of brown paper, to prevent the outer surface of the cake from becoming dry during the baking period. Bake the rich fruit cake at 275°F. for 3 to 3½ hours (the light fruit cake at 325°F. for about 2 hours). The cake should be made at least a couple of days before it is covered with almond icing.

Prepare the surface of the cake by trimming the top to allow it to sit flat on the cake board. Brush away any loose crumbs. Glaze the surface with unbeaten egg white or thinned and sieved apricot jam before covering with a thin coat of almond icing. Allow to stand overnight before covering with the fondant icing.

Divide the fondant paste in two. Colour one half by kneading a few drops of blue colouring into it.

Roll the white icing thinly, and after brushing the almond coat lightly with unbeaten egg white, cover the surface of the cake. Smooth with the palms of the hands, which have been dusted with sifted icing sugar, and trim the icing at the base of the cake. Leave until the following day before decorating.

The blue fondant is to be used for the panniers on the skirt. You will need seven panniers. Measure the distance from the centre of the cake to the hemline (with a Dolly Varden mould this will be about 5½ inches) and make a petal pattern of white paper or thin cardboard, 5½ inches long and about 3 inches wide in the centre. This pattern is for the panniers.

Place the pattern on the rolled fondant and cut round the pannier shape with a pointed knife. Cut seven of these. Arrange them slightly overlapping on the white icing, leaving a space in the centre for the rose trimming.

Allow the panniers to become quite dry before trimming with the lace edging.

Mass the roses down the centre of the doll's skirt, attaching them to the icing with a dab of royal icing through a plain writing tube.

Colour the rest of the icing green and brown and place alternate spoonfuls into an icing bag which has a number 17 leaf pipe attached. Fill in the spaces between the roses with the two-toned leaves.

Trim the doll top with lace and tulle and place it on top of the cake: you may have to cut a small section from the top to make the doll top secure.

Gather up some tulle with a sewing thread and make a hat. Trim it with a piped rose.

Tie a ribbon sash round the waist to complete the cake.

The panniers are cut from rolled fondant, using a pattern about 5½ inches long and 3 inches wide.

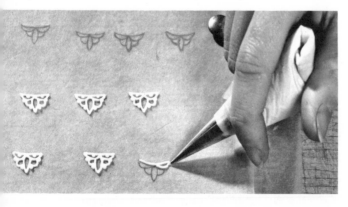

To make the lace fit neatly, pipe each piece with a slightly curved base.

Easter Bunny Cake

You will need:
> *A golden fruit cake, butter weight ½ lb., baked in an 8-inch round tin (recipe follows)*
> *1½ lb. fondant icing*
> *Egg white for glazing*
> *1 lb. almond paste (optional)*
> *Flooded bunnies*
> *Piped flowers*
> *One quantity of royal icing*
> *Food colourings*

Golden Fruit Cake

1 tablespoon butter
¼ cup golden syrup
½ cup brandy
8 oz. glacé pineapple
4 oz. glacé cherries
4 oz. glacé apricots
4 oz. mixed peel
8 oz. sultanas
4 oz. ground almonds
8 oz. butter
8 oz. light brown sugar
Grated rind of an orange

An Easter bunny decorates this attractive Easter Holiday cake. The figures are flooded, then attached to the cake.
Shown in colour on page 105

Grated rind of a lemon
4 eggs
10 oz. plain flour
A good pinch of salt
½ level teaspoon baking powder
1 level teaspoon each cinnamon and ginger

Line an 8-inch round tin with two thicknesses of white and two of brown paper. Preheat the oven to 275°F.

Combine the one tablespoon butter with the golden syrup and brandy in a saucepan and stir over the heat until both the butter and golden syrup have melted. Bring to the boil, then let it simmer for 3 minutes. Cool.

Cut the pineapple, cherries and apricots into uniform-sized pieces and mix the peel and sultanas.

Beat the butter and sugar to a light cream and add the grated orange and lemon rind. Add the eggs one at a time, beating well after each addition. Stir in the ground almonds.

Add half the fruit, then half the brandy syrup. Sift the flour with the salt, baking powder, cinnamon and ginger and add half to the mixture.

Add the remaining fruit, then the rest of the syrup. Lastly stir in the remaining flour and blend thoroughly.

Place in the prepared tin and bake at 275°F. for 3 to 3½ hours. Cool, wrap, and store the cake for at least a week before you cover it.

If you are going to have almond icing as well as fondant on this cake, brush the surface with unbeaten egg white or thinned and sieved apricot jam and cover with the rolled almond icing, dusting your hands with sifted icing sugar and making sure the covering is smooth. Trim the base and allow the cake to stand for several days before covering it with fondant.

Whether the fondant is put straight onto the cake or over the almond covering, use the same method of applying it as for the almond icing. Trim the base and leave till the following day before decorating.

Decorating the Cake

To make the flooded bunnies, place the bunny outline on a board and cover it with a sheet of waxed paper. Pin in position with paper pins. Using royal icing through a fine writing tube, trace the outline in white icing and leave until dry.

Using the same royal icing thinned down with a little water or lemon juice, and tinted according to your own colour scheme, fill in the outline, easing the icing into the smaller sections with a fine watercolour brush. Allow to become quite dry. This will take at least twenty-four hours.

To remove the bunnies, unpin the waxed paper, bring it to the edge of the board, and gently pull the paper away from the icing. With black colouring and a watercolour brush mark the rabbit's face, feet and tail and the check pattern on his trousers.

Attach the piped flowers and flooded bunny shapes to the cake with a little royal icing.

Use royal icing to flood the lettering and to pipe green leaves for the flowers.

To make a bunny, place waxed paper over the drawing, outline with a fine tube, then fill in with thinned down royal icing. Use a brush for the finer details.

31

Gipsy Caravan Cake

You will need:

A sultana cake, butter weight ½ lb., baked in a loaf tin (recipe follows)
1½ lb. almond paste
Egg white or apricot jam for glazing
A double quantity of royal icing
Food colourings
An 8-oz. packet of plain sweet 2-inch biscuits
Brown icing or brown crepe paper
Toy animals (optional)

Sultana Cake

8 oz. butter
8 oz. sugar
3 eggs
2 cups sultanas
¼ cup mixed peel
12 oz. plain flour
3 level teaspoons baking powder
A pinch of salt
1 level teaspoon mixed spice
1 level teaspoon nutmeg
3 tablespoons milk
3 tablespoons sherry

Neat and trim, the gipsy caravan is made from a sultana mixture and has a roof of almond paste. Shown in colour on page 105

You need a loaf tin measuring 9 by 5 by 3 inches. Line it with a layer of greased paper. Heat the oven to 325°F. Beat the butter and sugar to a soft cream and gradually add the well-beaten eggs. Stir in the sultanas and the chopped peel. Sift the flour with the baking powder, salt and spices and add to the mixture alternately with the milk and sherry.

Spoon the mixture carefully into the prepared tin and bake at 325°F. for two hours, or until a skewer inserted in the centre comes out clean. Remove from the tin and cool.

Decorating the Cake

To prepare the cake for covering, trim the top if necessary to shape the caravan roof, and brush away any loose crumbs. Glaze the top and sides with unbeaten egg white.

Take half the almond paste and roll it to about one-eighth of an inch in thickness. Measure the sides of the cake and cut the almond paste into four pieces the same height and length. Place them in position, trim the top and bottom edges and leave until the following day.

This almond paste gives a good surface for the piped royal icing, but if the cake is being prepared for a very young child, fondant paste may take the place of the almond paste on the sides. Use 12 oz. fondant and 12 oz. almond paste for the roof, shutters, door and steps.

Colour the royal icing red with food colouring. Using a number 22 basket tube, pipe vertical lines on the covered portion of the cake, leaving space at one end for the door, and on one side for the windows.

Add a few drops of red food colouring to the remaining 12 oz. of almond paste. Knead the colour in evenly. Place between two layers of waxed paper and roll out to an eighth of an inch in thickness.

Cut a rectangle 10 inches by 6 inches and mould it over the top of the cake to form the roof.

Now cut two pieces 1¾ by 1¼ inches. One of these pieces is cut to form the window and the other is cut in two to make the shutters.

Cut one more piece 2 inches by 1¼ inches to make the door; the top of this piece can be slightly rounded. Place these cut-outs on grease-proof paper to dry.

Knead the scraps of red almond paste together, then roll it out thinly. Cut strips from this to mould around pieces of pipe-cleaners or toothpicks to make the steps to the caravan door.

Now cut four rounds 1¼ inches in diameter to attach to the centre of the biscuits for the wheels. Then, using the scraps of paste, mould a chimney and attach it to the roof. It may be kept in position with a little of the royal icing.

Using a paper icing bag with a small hole and filled with some of the yellow royal icing, pipe the markings on the door, the shutters, and wheels, and scroll along the edge of the roof.

When the icing has set attach these smaller pieces to the cake.

Cover a board measuring 10 inches by 51 inches with brown crepe paper, or spread the board with brown icing. Sandwich four groups of 5 biscuits together with icing and place them down the centre of the board. Place the cake carefully on top of the biscuits, making sure it is evenly balanced.

Now place the steps and the wheels in position, securing them with royal icing.

Toy animals may be used to add interest.

Cut four rounds 1¼ inches in diameter from the re-rolled scraps of red almond paste. Attach to the biscuits with a little royal icing, and pipe the wheel spokes and the outline in yellow royal icing.

Duck Cake

A duck-shaped biscuit cutter is used to shape the main decoration on this cake. The water-lily is moulded from the same fondant icing.
Shown in colour on page 105

You will need:
   A light fruit cake or a marble cake of ½ lb. butter weight, baked in an 8-inch round cake tin (recipes on page 132)
   2 lb. white fondant icing
   Egg white for glazing
   Food colourings
   A duck-shaped biscuit cutter
   A fine watercolour brush
   Flower stamens
   One quantity of royal icing

Cut off about 2 oz. of the fondant and tint by working a few drops of pink colouring into it. Keep covered. This is for the water-lily.

Take another ounce of the fondant and add a little green colouring, working it in well. This is for the leaves.

Cut off another 4 oz. and colour it yellow. This is for the ducks.

Make the remainder of the fondant a pale blue

33

by kneading the colouring in evenly. This will be used for covering the cake.

Level the cake if necessary and brush the surface free from crumbs. Glaze lightly with unbeaten egg white. Roll the blue fondant into a round a little smaller than the cake, then lift it by rolling it round the rolling-pin and onto the cake. Smooth out the surface with the palms of the hands which have been dusted with icing sugar or cornflour. Ease the icing to the base of the cake, trim with a knife and leave until the following day before decorating.

The Ducks

Meanwhile, roll the yellow fondant thinly and, using a duck-shaped biscuit cutter, cut out seven ducks. Leave until dry, then with a brush dipped in either black or brown vegetable colouring, paint in the beak, eyes and wings.

Space five ducks at regular intervals round the cake, attaching them with a little royal icing. Place the remaining two ducks on top of the cake.

The Reeds and the Border

Divide the royal icing into three equal portions. Colour one blue, one green, and the other brown.

Using the brown royal icing in a number 1 writing tube, pipe the reeds mid-way between the ducks on the side of the cake, then with the green icing through the same sized tube, outline, then flood the reed leaves.

With some of the blue royal icing through a fine writing tube, make wavy lines under the ducks on the top of the cake and between the ducks on the side of the cake.

Make a rope border with the same blue icing through a fine star tube where the cake meets the covered board.

The Waterlily and Leaves

Roll out the pink fondant icing. Cut three or four sets of five petals, graduating them in size.

Curve each petal by placing it in the palm of the hand and lightly rubbing with the ends of a knitting needle or a modelling tool.

Allow the paste petals to dry, then assemble them in a flower shape, beginning with the larger outside petals and working towards the centre.

Place a small dab of yellow icing in the centre of each waterlily and press small stamens into the centre before the icing has dried.

For the leaves, roll, then cut these from the green coloured fondant. Mark the veins in the leaves while the fondant is still soft.

Attach the lily leaves and the flower to the cake with a dab of royal icing.

Maypole Cake

You will need:
> A marble cake baked in an 8-inch round cake tin (recipe on page 132)
> One quantity of snow frosting (recipe on page 57)
> Coloured fruit jubes, including half citrus shapes
> A long candle flower lighter or stick for the maypole mast
> A strap of licorice
> Coloured ribbons
> Food colouring

Tint the snow frosting with lemon food colouring and use it to frost the top and sides of the cake, swirling it to give a roughened effect. Allow to become set.

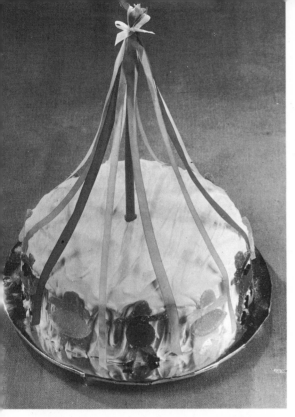

Now cut the coloured jubes into pieces, using the coloured illustrations as your guide. The girl's skirts are made from citrus jelly jubes. These are available from most health food shops. For the boy's figure, use round jelly jubes cut into slices.

Small pieces of licorice make the shoes and the caps. Attach the figures to the cake with the left-over scraps of snow frosting.

Cut coloured ribbons into equal lengths and attach them to the top of the coloured candle flower lighter or stick. Make a hole in the centre of the cake and insert the stick with the streamers.

Set the cake on a stand or on a board covered with coloured paper, and arrange the coloured ribbons to the cake between the little figures.

A marble cake mixture was used for this maypole birthday cake for a little girl. The dancing figures are made of sweets.
Shown in colour on page 106

Guardsman Cake

Cut the citrus jubes, fruit jubes, and pieces of licorice into shapes and form them into the dancing figures.

A guardsman cake for a small boy's birthday
Shown in colour on page 106

35

A four- to six-year-old boy would love this Changing of the Guard cake for his birthday.

You will need:

>A light fruit cake baked in an 8-inch square cake tin (recipe follows)
>Some gingerbread biscuit mixture (recipe follows)
>Some butter cream (recipe follows)
>One quantity of royal icing
>Green coconut
>Food colourings
>Marshmallow and chocolate
>Licorice
>Coloured barley sugar discs
>Coloured jubes

First of all you will need the recipes for the cake, the gingerbread biscuit mixture, and the butter cream.

Light Fruit Cake

>9 oz. butter
>9 oz. sugar
>4 eggs
>5 tablespoons milk
>1½ lb. mixed fruit
>Grated rind of an orange
>Grated rind of half a lemon
>2¼ level teaspoons baking powder
>1 rounded teaspoon nutmeg or mixed spice
>12 oz. plain flour
>A pinch of salt

Line the tin with two thicknesses of white paper. Beat the butter and sugar to a soft cream and then beat in the eggs, one at a time, until thoroughly mixed. Add the milk, then stir in the mixed fruit and the orange and lemon rind. Sift the flour with the baking powder, nutmeg and salt and stir into the mixture.

Bake in a moderate oven, 325°F., for about 2¼ hours. Leave until the following day.

Gingerbread Biscuit Mixture

>6 oz. butter or margarine
>4 oz. sugar
>1 egg
>2 tablespoons water
>½ teaspoon vanilla essence
>12 oz. plain flour
>1 level teaspoon baking powder
>1 rounded teaspoon ground ginger

Cream together the butter and sugar and add the beaten egg, water and vanilla. Sift the dry ingredients together and stir into the butter mixture, making a rather firm dough. Turn onto a board and knead only until smooth on the outside. Chill well.

Butter Cream

>2 oz. butter
>4 oz. sifted icing sugar
>Vanilla essence

Beat the butter to a soft cream, then gradually beat in the sifted icing sugar. Flavour with vanilla.

Assembling the Cake

Cut the fruit cake in halves. From the top of each half cut a wedge-shaped piece to form the peaked roof of the guardhouse. Spread a little butter cream on one side of the pieces of cut cake and join them back to back to make the square guard-house.

Remove the gingerbread dough from the refrigerator and roll to about three-eighths of an inch in thickness. Lift it carefully onto a shallow greased tray.

Using cardboard templates that you have made, cut out the shapes for the front of the guardhouse, the roof and the soldiers. Remove the surplus dough from the tray.

Bake in a moderate oven for about 10 minutes. Cool on the tray. Re-roll the scraps of pastry and cut out the remainder of the guardsmen. Bake as above.

Decorating the Cake

Thin down some red royal icing and flood or frost the guards' tunics. When this is dry, frost the trousers with royal icing coloured blue. Melt chocolate and use for the busbies. Use small pieces of marshmallow for the hands, and with the watercolour brush feather in the guards' busbies. Use licorice for the belt, boots and rifle.

Make a paper icing bag with greaseproof paper and, using white royal icing, add the final trim with a fine writing tube, making the buttons and band on the tunic.

Red and blue icing through the same type of bag provide the eyes and mouth.

Cover the front of the cake with some of the butter cream. Place the biscuit doorway in position.

Now prepare the roof. You will have two

pieces of gingerbread pastry, each one 3 inches square. Spread each with a little butter cream and overlap the barley sugar discs on each to represent the tiles. Spread a little more butter cream on the top of the cake and place the roof in position. Cover the ridge capping with coloured gum-drops.

Scatter green coconut on a large flat serving plate and place the guard-house in the centre. Spread a little of the butter cream on the back of the iced guards and set them in position on either side of the doorway and on both sides of the house. Make a border round the edge of the plate with coloured gum-drops.

The front and roof of the guardhouse and the toy soldiers are cut from gingerbread dough on the baking tray with the aid of cardboard or paper templates.

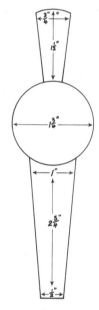

The pattern for the guardsmen. The figures are baked, then decorated.

Cutting out the guardhouse: to avoid extra handling place the rolled dough on the shallow baking tray before cutting out, and remove the surplus dough.

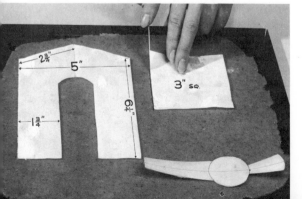

The baked figures of the guardsmen are decorated with blue trousers, red jackets, and white icing trim. Pieces of marshmallow, licorice, and melted chocolate are used as well.

Piping the guardsman's jacket: use white royal icing through a fine writing tube. 37

Drum Cake

A drum cake with a strictly masculine air for a small boy's birthday.
Shown in colour on page 106

Every small boy likes to beat on a drum. Let your special little boy celebrate his birthday with a novelty cake in the form of a drum. A light fruit cake mixture has been used for the large cake and the small drum in the centre, with little drums on the outer edge made of almond paste. You will need:

> *A light fruit cake, ½ lb. butter weight, baked in an 8-inch round cake tin (recipe on page 132) plus one extra quarter of the same mixture baked in a 3-inch round tin (for details see text below)*
>
> *2 lb. fondant icing*
> *A double quantity of royal icing*
> *Egg white for glazing*
> *Red and yellow food colouring*
> *¼ lb. almond paste*
> *Toy musicians*

Make up one and a quarter quantity of the light fruit cake mixture—that is, 10 oz. butter weight. Take enough of it to two-thirds fill a 3-inch round cake tin: this is for the small drum on top of the cake. Place the main quantity of mixture in an 8-inch round cake tin. Bake both cakes at 325°F. The small cake will take 50 to 60 minutes to cook; the larger one 2¼ hours.

Take a little more than half the fondant icing and use to cover the 8-inch cake, first brushing the cake with unbeaten egg white. Trim the base and place the cake on a covered board. Leave to become set and dry.

Take about one-third of the remaining fondant and use to cover the smaller cake, first brushing with egg white the same way. Leave it to set and dry also.

Meanwhile, cut the almond paste into six pieces and shape each piece into a drum. Cover these with the remainder of the rolled white fondant. Leave to set and dry.

Gather up the scraps of fondant icing, add red colouring, kneading in evenly, then roll the fondant thinly and cut into strips. The strips for the large cake should be half an inch wide, and those for the smaller drums need only be about a quarter of an inch wide.

Lightly brush the red strips with a little unbeaten egg white and arrange two bands round each drum.

Tint about 2 tablespoons of royal icing with some yellow colouring and, using a number 0 or 1 writing tube, decorate the large drum as shown in the colour picture.

Using white royal icing through the same size tube, lattice the top of each of the smaller drums and dot the space between the red bands.

Still with the same icing and tube, completely cover the top of the cake with a lattice design.

Change to a number 8 star tube and pipe a double vandyke in a star pattern round the sides of the large cake.

Fill in the spaces between the vandyke with vertical lines through a fine writing tube.

Pipe a double shell pattern round the edge of the large cake, and repeat the same pattern at the base of the cake.

Make sure the piped icing is perfectly dry before placing the larger drum in position.

From scraps of fondant icing mould the drumsticks, using toothpicks as a foundation. These may be decorated with a little of the yellow icing.

Set the small drums at regular intervals round the top of the cake and, for an effective decoration, add toy musicians on the board round the cake.

38

After the bands of red almond paste are placed in position, royal icing is piped through a fine writing tube to decorate the large drum for the centre of the cake.

Brush the sides of the cake with unbeaten egg white. Roll the fondant thinly. Measure the depth of the sides of the cake, then cut a strip of the fondant to fit round the cake. Place it in position. Trim the base with a knife and leave to become firm before rolling the remainder of the icing to make a scalloped trim for the base and the top or inside edge of the cake.

Place the covered cake on a board which has been covered with silver or gold paper. Re-roll the blue icing and cut a strip about $1\frac{1}{4}$ inches wide. Mark this with a cutter to make a scalloped edge and place in position at the base of the cake. Make another strip to use on the top edge of the cake.

Allow to set before trimming each scallop with a lacy pattern made with white royal icing through a number 00 writing tube.

The Lid

This does not contain any cake and is purely ornamental.

Take a piece of thin white cardboard and cut out a heart shape, using as a pattern the cake tin in which the cake was baked. Now cut a strip of the same cardboard about $1\frac{1}{4}$ inches wide. Attach

Chocolate Box Cake

You will need:
>A rich fruit cake, butter weight $\frac{1}{2}$ lb., baked in a 7-inch heart-shaped tin (recipe on page 133)
>1 lb. blue fondant icing
>$\frac{1}{2}$ lb. almond paste
>Egg white and apricot jam for glazing
>One quantity of royal icing
>Pink and white forget-me-nots
>Chocolates
>Ribbon
>Thin cardboard and adhesive tape

Bake the cake at 275°F. for $3\frac{1}{2}$ to 4 hours. Leave for several days before decorating.

Smooth the surface and if necessary brush the cake free from crumbs. Glaze with unbeaten egg white or thinned and sieved apricot jam. Roll the almond paste thinly and cover the top and sides of the cake. Trim the base and leave the icing to dry for a few days before covering with the fondant.

Real chocolates decorate the top of this heart-shaped chocolate box cake. The lid is purely for decoration.
Shown in colour on page 107

39

the strip to the heart shape to form the lid of the box, sticking it together with adhesive tape.

Cover the cardboard shape with royal icing and leave overnight to dry. Meanwhile outline the heart shape of the tin on a piece of paper and over it draw a diamond pattern, with each diamond about 1½ inches across. Trace the pattern onto the iced lid.

Using blue royal icing through a number 1 writing tube, outline the diamonds. When they have dried, thin down some of the royal icing with water or lemon juice and flood in each diamond pattern. Allow to dry.

Again with royal icing, this time a little thicker than the first and coloured blue, re-flood every second diamond. This gives a raised or quilted effect to the icing. Allow to become quite dry, then pipe tiny scallops, using a number 00 tube, round every diamond.

In every unraised diamond set seven little forget-me-nots to form a daisy. Trim the lid with a bow of ribbon.

Making the lid: with the heart-shaped baking tin as a guide, cut out the cardboard shape for the lid, attach a strip for the edge, and mark the diamond pattern in pencil before icing.

Arranging the Chocolates

Using a little royal icing secure some paper confectionery cases to the top of the cake, then, to keep the chocolates in position, place a dab of icing in each paper case.

Arrange the chocolates on top of the cake, set the trimmed lid at an angle, and the cake is complete.

Porcupine Cake

Porcupine cake: it's a fun cake, and not really prickly. The baby porcupines are made from the scraps of left-over cake.

You will need:
> A sponge or a butter cake mixture baked in two 8-inch sandwich tins (*sponge recipe on page 132*).
> One quantity of chocolate butter cream
> 4 oz. almonds
> Small pieces of licorice

Join the two layers of cake with some of the butter cream or with a berry or sharp-flavoured jam. Cut it down the centre, making two even halves.

Place the two halves together with the cut side down and sandwich them together with a little more of the butter cream or jam. This makes the body of the porcupine, which is now ready to shape: the three sketches will help to describe what you do.

 1. 2.

3.

Using a broad-bladed sharp knife, shave off pieces of cake from one end of each of the two halves, making them very pointed.

Using chocolate butter cream completely cover the surface of the cake. Smooth it neatly round the pointed end for the porcupine's face, and rough up the body with a fork.

Place the almonds in a saucepan and cover them with cold water. Bring to the boil; boil for one or two minutes. Drain, remove the brown skins, then dry the almonds thoroughly.

Cut each almond into lengths the width of a matchstick and stick them all over the porcupine's body to resemble bristles.

Cut two round pieces of licorice for the eyes and attach another piece of licorice, which has been shaved to a point, for the nose.

Set the porcupine on a flat platter covered with green coconut. The two baby porcupines in the picture were made the same way, using small pieces of cake.

Tinting the coconut. Place a cup of coconut in a bowl and add a few drops of green colouring. Rub the colouring into the coconut as you would rub butter into flour when making pastry. Place in a screw-topped bottle and shake well.

Clock Cake

You will need:
> *A sponge sandwich mixture baked in two 8-inch tins (recipe on page 132)*
> *One quantity of Vienna icing (recipe on page 131).*
> *One quantity of glace icing*
> *4 oz. chopped nuts*
> *Licorice strips*
> *A piped flower*
> *Food colouring*

A clock cake for a child's birthday. Set the hands to tell the child's age.

Join the two layers of the sponge with some of the Vienna icing. Add a few drops of pink colouring to the glacé icing and pour over the cake. Allow to become set.

Use the remainder of the Vienna icing to coat the sides of the cake, then press the chopped nuts into the icing.

Use small pieces of licorice for the numbers on the clock face, making them between $\frac{1}{2}$ and $\frac{3}{4}$ inch long. Cut the "hands" of the clock from licorice, too.

Both the hands and the numbers may be placed on the cake while the icing is still soft; or wait until it dries, then attach them with a little icing.

The hands may be placed to denote the child's age.

A small flower in the centre covers the joins of the clock hands.

Wagon Train

Cutting the chocolate cake and assembling the wagons.

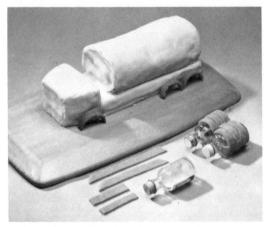

Sponge rollettes form the cabin, chocolate cake the base, and biscuits the wheels.

A wagon train for a little boy: the leading wagon can be named after the birthday boy. Shown in colour on page 107

You will need:

    A packet of chocolate cake mix
    A packet of sponge rollettes
    1 lb. almond paste
    Egg white or apricot jam for glazing
    Half quantity of chocolate butter icing
    2 dozen biscuits, $1\frac{1}{2}$ inches in diameter
    One quantity of royal icing
    Green coconut
    Licorice and black crochet cotton
    Toy horses and drivers

Make up the cake mix according to the directions given on the packet and bake either in an oblong Swiss roll tin or in two square 7-inch sandwich tins. Cool.

Leave until the following day before shaping: the cake will be easier to handle.

Cut the chocolate cake into pieces $3\frac{1}{2}$ inches long and 2 inches wide. Frost these with chocolate butter icing and leave to set.

Knead the almond paste on a board, using a little sifted icing sugar to prevent it from sticking. Roll it out thinly and cut it into six pieces. Each

piece should be large enough to cover the little jam rollettes, and extend about $\frac{1}{2}$ inch at each end for the opening to the wagon.

Brush them lightly with unbeaten egg white or thinned and sieved apricot jam and cover each jam rollette to represent a wagon top.

Place one on each frosted wagon base, flush with the rear but leaving a small seat area in front.

From the remainder of the chocolate cake cut two pieces for each wagon, each the same width as the base, but only $\frac{1}{2}$ inch wide. These pieces of cake form the axles. They are not seen on the finished cake as they are covered by the wheels, but they lift the wagon from ground level.

Using the plain sweet biscuits decorated with

red royal icing to represent the spokes, make and attach the wheels, four for each wagon. A dab of royal icing will hold them securely in place.

Arrange the completed wagons on a board covered with green coconut, and for a more realistic effect place toy drivers and toy horses in their relative positions.

The horses' harness is made with thin strips of licorice, and the reins from heavy black crochet cotton.

Write the birthday boy's name on the leading wagon.

Hat-box Cake

An enchanting hat-box for a fashionable young lady not yet in her teens. You will need:

A rainbow mixture baked in two 7-inch sand-
wich tins and one 8-inch sandwich tin
(recipe follows)
1 lb. fondant icing
Egg white for glazing
One quantity of thin royal icing
One quantity of royal icing of piping con-
sistency
Ribbon
Moulded flowers
Piped forget-me-nots
Tiny birthday candles
Corks and small piped flowers

Rainbow Cake

8 oz. butter
8 oz. sugar
1 teaspoon vanilla essence
3 eggs
8 oz. self-raising flour
4 oz. plain flour
$\frac{3}{4}$ cup milk
A good pinch of salt
Food colouring
2 level tablespoons cocoa

Cream together the butter and sugar until light and fluffy. Flavour with vanilla and gradually add the well-beaten eggs. Sift the flours with the salt and add to the mixture alternately with the milk. Divide into three portions, one slightly larger than the other two.

A rainbow mixture was used for this attractive
novelty hat-box cake for a very young miss.
Shown in colour on page 108

Sift the cocoa into one of the smaller portions, add pink colouring to the second, and leave the larger portion plain.

Place the chocolate and pink mixtures in the well-greased 7-inch tins and the plain mixture in the 8-inch tin.

Bake in a moderate oven, 350°F., for 20 to 25 minutes. Turn out and allow to cool.

Frosting and Decorating the Cake

Join the two 7-inch cakes with butter cream (see page 36). Divide the fondant icing in two, and roll half to cover the sides only of the joined layers of rainbow cake, but before placing it on the cake brush it with unbeaten egg white. Use the remainder of the fondant to cover the 8-inch cake, which will become the lid of the hat-box: it should also be brushed with egg white before it is placed on the cake. Extend the icing a little deeper than the sides of this cake. Allow to become firm, if necessary overnight.

Take the thin royal icing (use lemon juice to thin it down), and divide it into two. Colour one half a pale pink and use it to ice the sides of the double layer cake. Coat the lid cake with the white icing. Allow both to dry.

Using a number 22 icing tube and white royal icing make stripes about three-quarters of an inch apart on the pink iced cake. Trim each stripe with piped forget-me-nots.

43

Scatter, then secure more forget-me-nots on the lid of the hat-box, using tiny dabs of royal icing.

Secure a band of ribbon across the top of the lid and trim it with moulded roses and leaves.

Using a fine writing tube, or a fine paper cone, decorate the edge of the lid with a scroll design. When the icing is dry, place the lid in position and set the cake on the covered board or on a mirror.

The Candle Holders

For these you will need medium-sized corks, candles and small piped flowers.

Hollow out the narrow end of each cork slightly and, using a lighted match, melt the end of each candle before placing it in the indentation you have made in the cork.

Decorate the cork with tiny piped flowers, using a little royal icing to make them stick. A dab of the same icing will keep the corks in position round the base of the cake.

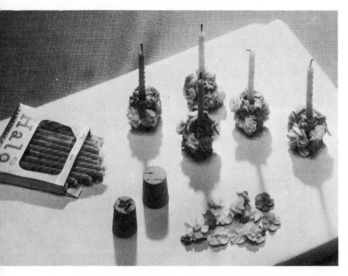

Piped sugar flowers cover small corks to form pretty holders for the birthday candles.

Gingerbread Children

You will need:
> *One quantity of gingerbread biscuit mixture*
> *(recipe follows)*
> *One quantity of royal icing*
> *Cardboard cut-outs*
> *Assorted food colourings*

Gingerbread Biscuit Mixture

3 oz. butter
3 oz. brown sugar
1 egg
1 tablespoon golden syrup
$\frac{1}{4}$ level teaspoon bicarbonate of soda
1 teaspoon milk
8 oz. plain flour
$\frac{1}{2}$ level teaspoon ground ginger
$\frac{1}{2}$ level teaspoon cinnamon

Cream the butter and sugar well together. Add the beaten egg and then the golden syrup. Dissolve the soda in the milk and add. Sift the flour and spices and add to the mixture, mixing to a firm dough. Turn onto a floured board and knead only until smooth on the outside.

If time permits, chill the mixture for several hours before rolling out.

Divide the dough into eight pieces and roll one piece at a time into 6-inch squares. As soon as it has been rolled place each square on a shallow greased biscuit tray.

With thin cardboard templates made from the following diagram, cut out the shapes by placing each on the rolled dough on the baking tray and running a thin, sharp-pointed knife round the outline.

Remove the excess dough from the tray and bake the biscuits two at a time in a moderate oven for about 10 or 12 minutes.

Lift them from the tray with an egg slice and cool them on a wire cooler.

Making the Templates

Using one-inch graph paper (or draw one-inch squares on plain paper) draw up two 6-inch squares.

Using these drawings as your guide, draw an outline of the girl and boy on the paper. Trace each one onto a thin piece of cardboard and cut out the shape with either a razor blade or fine pointed scissors.

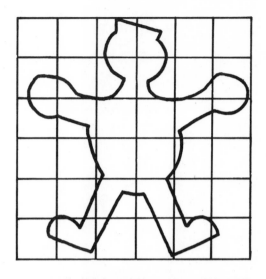

Gingerbread children are dressed in gay icing colours to delight your little party guests. Shown in colour on page 108

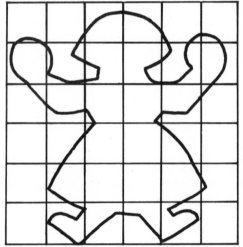

The shapes for the gingerbread children, cut out as templates

Decorating the Figures

Divide and tint the royal icing according to your own style. The little girl's dress and the boy's trousers have been flooded with royal icing thinned down with lemon juice.

Use the royal icing of pipe-work consistency to add the decorative touches to the costumes.

Easter Bonnets

You will need:
> *One quantity of biscuit pastry (recipe follows)*
> *One quantity of marshmallow (recipe follows)*
> *Apricot jam for glazing*
> *One quantity of royal icing*
> *Piped flowers*

Biscuit Pastry

> 3 oz. butter
> 3 oz. sugar
> 1 egg yolk
> 1 tablespoon cold water
> $\frac{1}{2}$ teaspoon vanilla essence or $\frac{1}{2}$ teaspoon grated orange or lemon rind
> A pinch of salt
> 6 oz. plain flour
> $\frac{1}{2}$ level teaspoon baking powder

Beat the butter and sugar to a soft cream and add the egg yolk, cold water and either vanilla essence or grated rind. Mix again. Sift the salt with the flour and baking powder and stir into the butter mixture, making a rather firm dough. Turn onto a floured board and knead only until smooth on the outside.

Roll to an eighth of an inch in thickness and cut into rounds with a 3-inch fluted cutter. Place on a greased shallow tray and bake in a moderate oven, 350°F., for 12 to 15 minutes. Makes about $1\frac{1}{2}$ dozen.

45

Marshmallow

1 cup sugar
1 tablespoon liquid glucose
¾ cup boiling water
1 level tablespoon gelatine
½ teaspoon vanilla essence
Pink and lemon food colourings

Combine the sugar with the glucose and add half the boiling water. Stir until both the sugar and glucose have dissolved. Add the remainder of the water to the gelatine and stir until the gelatine has dissolved. If necessary, heat this mixture over a gentle heat.

Combine the two mixtures in a bowl, beat to mix well, then allow to cool slightly. Add the vanilla and beat at high speed until the marshmallow is thick and white, about 20 minutes. Divide the mixture into three parts. Colour one pink, another lemon, and leave the remainder white. Spoon the mixture into well-greased gem irons and allow to become firm and set.

Assembling the Bonnets

Glaze the top of each cooked and cooled biscuit a little to one side with thinned and sieved apricot jam, then place a marshmallow on each to form the crown of the hat. Using coloured royal icing pipe a band round each hat and press some small piped flowers into the icing as a decoration. A few piped green leaves will add to its attractiveness.

Marshmallows on home-made biscuits make pretty little Easter bonnets. Trim as you like with piped or moulded flowers.

Birthday Express

This express train has been designed for the small boy of the family so that there will be a truck for each little guest to take home. Our cake mixture allows for five small cakes, but you can adjust the number according to the size of the party. You will need:

A plain cake mixture baked in three tins as given in the recipe below
Glacé icing, using 1½ lb. icing sugar
Coloured coconut
Licorice straps
Coloured Lifesaver sweets
Brightly coloured sweets
Nuts
A toy train
Piped daisies
One quantity of royal icing

Plain Cake

8 oz. butter
8 oz. sugar
4 eggs
1 teaspoon vanilla essence
9 oz. self-raising flour
5 oz. plain flour
About ¾ cup milk

A toy train decorates this birthday cake for a 5-year-old. There's a truck for each small guest to take home.
Shown in colour on page 108

Cream the butter and sugar together until light and fluffy. Add the well-beaten eggs a little at a time, then flavour with vanilla.

Sift the flours together and add them to the mixture alternately with the milk. Stir until smooth.

Divide the mixture between two well-greased 7-inch square sandwich tins and one 10-inch by 3-inch by 2-inch bar tin. Bake the cakes at 350°F., allowing 25 minutes for the cakes in the sandwich tins and about 35 to 40 minutes for the bar tin.

Make the cakes the day before they are to be decorated.

Shaping and Decorating the Cake

From the two square cakes cut five 2½-inch squares. Prepare the glacé icing, but take out one-third and colour it a pale green, then heat it slightly. It is used to coat the bar cake and one of the small cakes.

While the bar cake icing is still soft, press coloured coconut into the sides and arrange two long strips of licorice on the top for the train lines.

Divide the remaining two-thirds of glacé icing into four equal portions. Colour each a different pastel shade and use to coat the remaining four squares of cake. Allow to set.

For each of the small trucks cut strips of licorice to attach to the sides, placing them about half an inch from the bottom of the cake. Place a coloured Lifesaver at each end of the strip for the truck wheels.

Fill the trucks with coloured sweets, nuts or

a mixture of both, and add a flag with the little guest's name.

Decorate the edge of the train line on the bar cake with small piped flowers and a few piped leaves. Write "Happy Birthday" in royal icing across the top and add a shell border with the same icing at the base.

Set a toy train complete with candles on top of the bar cake.

Little Cakes for a Children's Party

Sailing ships, little ducklings, and small iced cakes for a children's party.
Shown in colour on page 109

As fresh cake crumbles easily and is difficult to cut into fancy shapes, plan to make the basic mixture the day before you intend icing the cakes.

Choose a good basic butter cake recipe and bake it either in patty tins or in a slab or lamington tin.

You may use either butter icing or royal icing for the decorations, but the covering icing is usually a soft glacé icing.

Miniature marzipan fruits, sugar flowers either piped or moulded, or piped designs with royal icing are suggestions for decorating.

A coating of finely chopped nuts or of plain, toasted or coloured coconut may be used on the sides of these small cakes. This coating is added before the covering icing has dried.

For special party cakes, or petit-fours, it is suggested that each cake be brushed with jam and then covered with a very thin layer of almond icing before the glacé icing is added. The almond layer is not entirely necessary, but as well as adding richness and flavour to the cakes, it gives a completely smooth and even coat on which to work with the glacé icing and then the decorations.

Plain Cake

This plain cake mixture has been used for the little drums, the petit-fours, and the little sailing-ships.

> 8 oz. butter
> 8 oz. sugar
> 3 eggs
> 1 teaspoon vanilla essence
> 8 oz. plain flour
> 4 oz. self-raising flour
> ¾ cup milk

Cream together the butter and sugar until light and fluffy. Gradually add the well-beaten eggs and flavour with vanilla. Sift together the plain and the self-raising flour and add to the mixture alternately with the milk.

Place the mixture in a well-greased 9-inch square cake tin which has been lined on the bottom with greased paper, and bake at 350°F. for about 40 to 45 minutes. Turn out and allow to cool.

Glacé Icing

> 1 lb. sifted icing sugar
> 6 to 7 tablespoons water or fruit juice
> Food colourings

Place the sifted icing sugar in a saucepan. Add the water or fruit juice and stir with a wooden spoon until smooth. Colour as desired. Heat briefly over a low heat, then use to cover the cakes. During the icing of a number of cakes, keep the glacé icing standing in a container of hot water to prevent it hardening.

SAILING SHIPS

You will need:
> *One quantity of plain cake mixture baked in a 9-inch square cake tin (recipe on this page)*
> *One quantity of glacé icing (see this page)*
> *½ lb. almond paste*
> *One quantity of royal icing*
> *Ice cream wafers*
> *Food colourings*
> *Apricot jam for glazing*

Using a pattern cut from light cardboard, or a boat-shaped cutter, cut the shapes for the boats from the plain cake square.

Brush each one with thinned and sieved apricot jam and cover with thinly rolled almond paste.

Divide the glacé icing into as many colours as required, then completely cover each cake with glacé icing. Allow to become set and dry.

Decorate the sides of each boat with royal icing, using a fine writing tube or a fine star tube.

Cut the ice cream wafers in the shape of sails and attach them to the cakes with a little royal icing.

LITTLE DRUMS

You will need:
> *One quantity of plain cake mixture baked in a 9-inch square cake tin (recipe on this page)*
> *½ lb. almond paste*
> *One quantity of glacé icing (see this page)*
> *One quantity of royal icing (see page 7)*
> *Red food colouring*
> *Apricot jam and egg white for glazing*
> *Toothpicks*

Using a 2-inch round cutter, cut shapes from the plain square cake. Brush the top and sides of each little cake with apricot jam that has been thinned and sieved.

Roll the almond paste thinly and cut into strips for the sides of the little drums. Place the strips of paste round each drum and trim any surplus from the top and the bottom.

Colour the rest of the almond paste red with food colouring, then roll it thinly. Cut strips ¼ inch wide to use as bands on the sides of the cakes. Brush the strips with unbeaten egg white and place one at the top and another at the base of each cake.

Make up the white glacé icing and carefully ice the top of each drum. Allow to dry.

Make drumsticks by covering wooden toothpicks with plain almond paste and tipping them with red almond paste.

Cross the sticks on top of each cake, then, using royal icing coloured yellow, add the cord trim on the sides.

LITTLE DUCKLINGS

It takes only a little imagination to turn small cakes baked in deep patty tins, and some of the same mixture baked in a round flat tin, into little ducklings to add fun to the children's party table.

It is best to bake the cakes the day before they are to be shaped and iced: they may crumble if they are too fresh.

Basic Mixture

4 oz. butter
4 oz. sugar
2 eggs
8 oz. self-raising flour
A pinch of salt
½ cup milk
½ teaspoon vanilla essence

Beat the butter and sugar to a soft cream. Gradually add the well-beaten eggs, beating well. Sift the flour and salt and add to the mixture alternately with the milk and essence.

Two-thirds fill six well-greased deep patty tins and spread the remainder of the mixture in a greased 7-inch sandwich tin.

Bake at 350°F. The patty cakes will take about 20 minutes, and the mixture in the sandwich tin about 30 minutes.

Shaping and Decorating the Ducklings

As well as the patty cakes and the round cakes you will need:

> Coconut
> Yellow, black (or brown) and green food colouring
> About ½ cup apricot jam
> 2 tablespoons water
> 2 oz. almond paste
> Miniature umbrellas (optional)

Using scissors trim the cakes which were baked in the deep patty tins, making one side pointed to represent the tail. From the cake made in the round tin, using a 1-inch plain round cutter, cut six rounds for the duckling's head.

Thin down the apricot jam with a little water, boiling it for two or three minutes, then allowing it to cool. Place a few drops of yellow colouring in the coconut and rub it with the fingers until the coconut is evenly coloured.

With thinned apricot jam, brush the rounds for the head and the body shapes, then roll them in the yellow coconut. Place the piece for each head in position using a little jam to make it stick.

Colour half the almond paste green and the remainder yellow. Mould the green almond paste to make the boy ducklings' caps and the girl ducklings' neck-bands. Roll the remainder of the green paste and cut with small fluted cutters for the girl ducklings' hats.

Mould the pieces of yellow almond paste for the eyes and beaks, or use two pieces of blanched almond for each beak. For the eyes, paint a brown or black centre on the yellow paste, and draw lines with the same food colouring on the boy ducklings' caps.

The miniature umbrellas, which may be bought from the party favour counter at most large city stores, are optional, but they add to the decorative appearance of these novelty cakes.

49

STORYBOOK COOKIES

Baking cookies like those in our colour picture is fun the whole family can enjoy. While the grown-ups make and roll the biscuit dough the children can cut out the shapes and have a hand in adding the decorations.

Because it isn't easy to buy cooky cutters in the shapes used here, trace our patterns on thin cardboard. To use them, place the cardboard cut-out on the biscuit dough and go round it with a sharp pointed knife.

In all biscuit decorations we have used royal icing.

Here is the recipe for the cooky dough:

- 6 oz. butter or margarine
- ¼ cup sugar
- 1 egg
- ⅓ cup ground almonds
- ¼ teaspoon almond essence
- 2½ cups plain flour and
- ½ level teaspoon baking powder
- (or 2 cups plain flour and
- ½ cup self-raising flour)

Beat the butter and sugar to a soft cream and gradually add the beaten egg. Stir in the ground almonds and the almond essence, then the sifted flour and baking powder.

Turn onto a lightly floured board and knead only until smooth on the outside. Roll thinly and cut into shapes. Place on a shallow greased tray and bake in a moderate oven (350 degrees F.) for 6 to 8 minutes. Allow them to cool slightly then remove from the tray. Ice and decorate them when they are cold.

Storybook cookies are fun for all the family to make.
Shown in colour on page 109

Telegram Cake for Dad

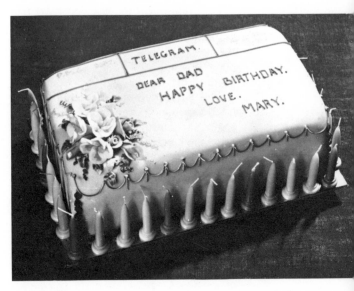

A telegram design makes a novel birthday cake for Dad.
Shown in colour on page 109

You will need:

A light fruit cake, butter weight ½ lb. (recipe on page 132), baked in an oblong tin 8 inches by 4½ inches (see text below)
1 lb. almond paste (optional)
Egg white and apricot jam for glazing
1 lb. fondant icing
One quantity of royal icing
Moulded or piped flowers or moulded fruits
Candles
Food colourings

If you haven't a tin measuring 8 inches by 4½ inches, bake the cake in an 8-inch square tin, let it stand for a few days, then cut a piece 3½ inches wide off one side. The cake is to be baked at a temperature of 300°F. for 2½ hours.

Brush the cake with unbeaten egg white or thinned and sieved apricot jam and cover with the rolled almond paste. Leave for two or three days, then brush with unbeaten egg white and cover with fondant tinted a pale lemon. Leave until the icing has set. Place on a covered board.

Colour some of the royal icing brown and the remainder a light green. With the brown icing

51

in a fine writing tube, rule out the telegram form, filling in the greeting with the same icing and tube.

Arrange a posy of moulded or piped flowers, or make an arrangement of moulded marzipan fruits. Attach to the cake with royal icing and add leaves and trails with a mixture of green and brown icing. This two-toned effect is obtained by placing alternate spoonfuls of green and brown icing in the same bag.

Using the same variegated icing pipe a single scallop with bar round the edge of the cake.

Shell-edge the bottom in brown icing and arrange the candles on the board round the cake.

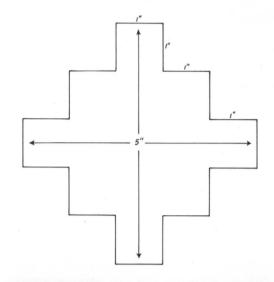

Grape and Lattice Cake

You will need:

> A rich fruit cake, butter weight $\frac{1}{2}$ lb., baked in an 8-inch square cake tin (recipe on page 133)
> Egg white and apricot jam for glazing
> 1 lb. almond paste
> 1$\frac{1}{2}$ lb. fondant icing, coloured pastel blue
> A double quantity of royal icing
> Food colourings

For this design it is best to have a perfectly flat surface, so either level the top of the cake or turn it upside down on the board, filling in the corners if necessary with scraps of almond paste.

Brush the surface with unbeaten egg white or thinned and sieved apricot jam and cover with the almond paste. When this has thoroughly dried, brush with unbeaten egg white and cover with the pastel blue fondant icing. Trim the base and allow the icing to become quite dry before decorating.

For the open section on top of the cake draw a 5-inch square on a piece of greaseproof paper. Make this into a squared design as shown. Each inner section should measure 1 inch. Prick or trace onto the cake.

Using a number 0 writing tube and some well-worked royal icing which has been coloured brown, lattice the area outside the squared design on top of the cake. Allow this to become quite dry.

Now add some purple colouring to the remainder of the royal icing, and pipe in grapes,

Lattice work in brown icing outlines the squared design on this cake. The grapes and leaves are piped with royal icing.
Shown in colour on page 110

leaves and tendrils round the edge of the cake and down the sides at the corners only.

The grapes are piped in purple and the leaves and tendrils in the same brown as was used for the lattice.

Change to a number 8 star tube and make an edging at the base of the cake where it meets the board.

If liked, a greeting or a name may be piped in the centre of the cake in brown or purple icing.

52

Say it with Flowers

A quaint idea for a decoration on a birthday cake is a gay cart filled with flowers.
Shown in colour on page 110

You will need:

A rich fruit cake, butter weight ½ lb., baked in an 8-inch square cake tin (recipe on page 133)
1 lb. almond paste
Egg white and apricot jam for glazing
1½ lb. fondant icing
One quantity of royal icing
1 yard narrow satin ribbon
Piped roses, jonquils and forget-me-nots
Food colourings

Cover the cake in the usual way with the almond paste, first brushing it with unbeaten egg white or thinned and sieved apricot jam. Let it stand for two or three days and then cover with fondant icing which has been tinted with a little lemon and a little pink colouring to give a magnolia shade. Leave until the icing is quite dry.

The cart design was borrowed from a birthday greeting card. First trace the outline of the cart on a piece of waxed paper, then lightly trace it through the paper by pricking the outline with a pin, or running a fine skewer round the shape.

Lift the waxed paper from the cake, then flood the wheels with softened royal icing (directions for flooding are given on page 61). Allow the flooded shapes to become perfectly dry, then outline the wheels with black royal icing through a number 00 tube, and pipe the spokes with the same icing.

Now pipe in the cart outline and let it dry before decorating with the piped flowers. A small dab of icing on the back of each flower will keep it in place.

Cut four pieces of the ribbon to cover the corners of the cake. Attach the ends to the cake with icing and decorate with flowers and leaves. Pipe a border with a number 8 star tube at the base of the cake and decorate each corner with a piped rose and two-toned leaves.

On a piece of waxed paper draw an oval outline, pipe it with a fine writing tube, then flood it with royal icing tinted the same colour as the fondant covering on the cake.

Allow it to dry before printing the name in the centre with black royal icing. When it has been placed in position on the cake, outline it with tiny leaves.

Yellow Rose Cake

You will need:

A rich fruit cake (three-quarters of the ½-lb. butter-weight mixture—recipe on page 133) baked in a 7-in. heart-shaped tin
1 lb. almond paste
Egg white and apricot jam for glazing
1 lb. fondant icing
Food colourings
A large moulded yellow rose
About 1 dozen moulded leaves
One quantity of royal icing

Remember that the fruit cake is a smaller one than usual (6 oz. butter and the other ingredients in proportion). Bake it at 300°F. for 3¼ hours. Leave for a few days before decorating.

Brush the cake free from any crumbs and glaze the surface lightly with unbeaten egg white or thinned and sieved apricot jam. Roll the almond paste and use it as a foundation icing for the cake. Allow to stand for several days.

53

Yellow rose cake: all-over stippling on a birthday cake for any age is most effective and reduces the amount of pipework.
Shown in colour on page 111

Use a lemon-coloured fondant icing or work a few drops of yellow into a pound of white fondant. Roll this evenly. Brush the almond coating with unbeaten egg white and cover with the fondant. Smooth the surface with the palms of the hands which have been dusted with sieved icing sugar, then trim the base with a large knife. Place on a covered board.

Using the left-over fondant mould one large rose for the centre of the cake. Add a little green colouring to the remaining fondant and when it has been well worked in, mould small pieces into leaf shapes. Leave these to dry over the handle of a wooden spoon.

Measure the distance round the cake and divide it into equal spaces. Cut a scallop pattern in paper to fit, then mark the position of the scallops on the cake by pricking lightly with a pin.

Tint the royal icing a pale yellow to match the covering icing.

Outline the scallops with this icing through a fine writing tube.

Trace the pointed scallops on a sheet of waxed paper and, using a number 00 tube, make three sets of lace to trim each scallop on the cake. Leave these overnight to dry.

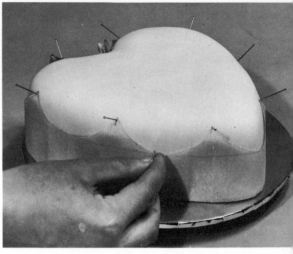

For the scallops, measure round the cake and mark at equal intervals, cut a scallop pattern to fit, then mark the scallop outline onto the cake with a skewer or prick it out with a pin.

The lace design for the yellow rose cake

Meanwhile, stipple the surface of the cake above the scallops on the sides, and completely covering the top. The royal icing should be the same consistency as you would have for lettering. Stippling does not follow any set pattern, but is a series of wavy lines. It is not necessary to follow a continuous line, either. The tube may be lifted at any time, but make sure you keep the waves and curves regular in size, with equal spaces between.

Make three or four tiny dots with royal icing where the lace-work is to go, then carefully place it in position. It should stand out slightly from the side of the cake.

Using a number 2 writing tube make a series of large dots at the base of the cake. Place the large moulded rose in the centre of the cake, securing it with a dab of royal icing, surround it with the green leaves and add two or three leaves on the side of the cake board to give the final touch.

Wisteria Cake

A simple spray of wisteria trims this pretty cake. Flooded lettering forms the name, and a string scallop with forget-me-nots makes the side decoration.
Shown in colour on page 111

You will need:
> *A rich fruit cake, butter weight ½ lb., baked in an 8-inch round cake tin (recipe on page 133)*
> *1 lb. almond paste*
> *1½ lb. fondant icing*
> *Egg white and apricot jam for glazing*
> *About one dozen piped wisteria flowers*
> *About 2½ dozen piped forget-me-nots*
> *One quantity of royal icing*
> *Food colourings*

This very simple design features pink and lilac wisteria with two-tone leaves.

Brush the cake free from crumbs and glaze the surface lightly with egg white or thinned and sieved apricot jam. Cover with almond paste. Let it stand for a few days to become quite dry. Glaze with unbeaten egg white and cover with the fondant, then allow to dry thoroughly before decorating.

For the dropped string work on the sides use a number 0 tube and royal icing, then break the line by placing two tiny forget-me-nots and tiny leaves at the base of each scallop.

The name, in flooded letters, balances the decorations on the top of the cake.

An attractive finish consists of piped stars of pink royal icing round the cake where it joins the covered board.

Posy Cake for Grandma

There's an old-world charm about this posy cake for Gran's birthday. Moulded flowers form the centre posy, and piped sweet pea buds are featured on the sides.
Shown in colour on page 111

55

You will need:

> A rich fruit cake, butter weight ½ lb., baked in an 8-inch cake tin (recipe on page 133)
> 1 lb. almond paste (optional)
> Egg white and apricot jam for glazing
> 2 lb. white fondant icing
> One quantity of royal icing
> 8 moulded frangipani flowers
> 8 pastel blue moulded roses
> 3 pink moulded roses and 3 lemon moulded roses
> 12 piped sweet pea buds
> 5 dozen forget-me-nots
> Food colourings

Brush the top and sides of the cake with a little unbeaten egg white or thinned and sieved apricot jam.

If almond paste is to be used as an under-covering, roll it into a round a little smaller than the cake. Lift on, smooth evenly with the hands which have been dusted with sifted icing sugar, then trim the base evenly. Set the cake aside for about a week.

Reserve about ¼ lb. of the fondant icing to make the moulded flowers.

Add a few drops of blue colouring to the main quantity of fondant and knead it on a board lightly dusted with icing sugar, making sure the colour is evenly blended. Roll out so that it is a little smaller than the cake. Glaze the surface of the cake with unbeaten egg white, then lift the fondant onto it carefully, smoothing with the palms of the hands which have been dusted with icing sugar. Trim away any excess from the base of the cake and lift onto the covered board. Allow to stand at least one day before decorating.

Divide the ¼ lb. fondant icing and mould the frangipani and the roses.

Take out a tablespoonful of the royal icing and colour it brown; place another tablespoonful in a small bowl and colour it green for the leaves; colour the remainder blue for the pipework and the forget-me-nots.

Using scraps of fondant icing make a small mound and place it in the centre of the cake. Arrange the moulded flowers on it, banking them in the centre.

Using a little of the royal icing in a writing tube, attach the sweet pea buds at regular intervals round the side of the cake. With the forget-me-nots spell out the name "Gran" or the children's favourite name for her, attaching them with the same icing.

With a number 0 writing tube pipe the birthday greeting in brown royal icing, then add a double scalloped curtain round the top edge with some of the blue royal icing.

Use a number 8 star tube for the shell border and a number 16 leaf tube or a paper cone for the leaves, which may be variegated by placing alternate teaspoonfuls of brown and green icing in the bag.

Flower Posy Cake

A flower posy cake allows a choice of pretty blooms for the centre. Tint the frosting to match one of the colours of the flowers.
Shown in colour on page 112

You have a choice of pretty centres for this cake. Tint the snow frosting that covers the fruit cake so that it matches the flowers in the Victorian posy. You will need:

56

A rich fruit cake, butter weight ½ lb., baked
in an 8-inch ring tin (recipe on page 133)
1 lb. fondant or almond icing (optional)
One quantity of snow frosting (recipe follows)
Small rosebuds piped on milliner's wire
Single blossoms, or silver or gold cachous
Tulle for the posy ruffle
A quantity of royal icing (for making roses
and attaching blossoms)

Bake the cake at 275°F. for 3½ hours. It should be made a few days before it is needed.

Whether the cake is covered first with a fondant icing or with almond icing is a matter of personal choice. Either will make a good base for the snow frosting, but it may be omitted.

Snow Frosting

2 cups sugar
½ cup water
2 dessertspoons liquid glucose
2 stiffly beaten egg whites
1 teaspoon vanilla essence
Food colouring

Combine the sugar, water and glucose in a saucepan and place over the heat, stirring lightly, until the sugar has dissolved. Boil to medium-ball stage (242°F. on a candy thermometer). Have the egg whites stiffly beaten in a bowl and slowly pour the hot sugar syrup over them, beating continually. Add the vanilla and the food colouring and continue beating at high speed until thick and creamy, about 10 minutes.

Completely cover the cake with the frosting, then run the back of the spoon several times from the base to the top to give a frosted appearance. Leave overnight to become quite set.

Decorating the Cake

Decorate the cake with single blossoms, attaching them with a little royal icing, or use gold or silver cachous to decorate.

The posy. It is easier to pipe rosebuds onto wire than to attach the wire after the roses have been made and dried. To make the base for a rose on wire, dip the ends of a piece of milliner's wire in thick royal icing, then leave to dry. Pipe the rose around this, using a small petal tube.

Set the cake on a board covered with silver or gold paper. Make a posy from the wired roses and set them in a ruffle of tulle. Place the posy in the centre of the cake.

Making the posy: instead of piping the roses on toothpicks, pipe them directly on wire. Add green royal icing for the calyx.

Basket of Roses

Choose your own colour scheme for this delightful basket of roses cake. The lid lifts off easily for cutting.
Shown in colour on page 112

57

You will need:
>A rich fruit cake, butter weight ½ lb., baked
>in an 8-inch round cake tin (recipe on
>page 133)
>1½ lb. cream-coloured fondant icing
>Egg white for glazing
>Moulded roses and leaves
>Light cardboard for the lid
>A ribbon bow
>Food colourings
>A double quantity of royal icing

Make the surface of the cake even, brush away any crumbs and lightly glaze with unbeaten egg white. Roll out the fondant and cover the surface of the cake. Trim the base and leave until the fondant has set.

Using left-over fondant icing mould about eight roses and a few rosebuds. Knead a little blue and green colouring into the cream-coloured fondant and you will have a green fondant from which you can shape the leaves.

Make up the double quantity of royal icing. Colour one-third of it a dark brown with vegetable colouring, and tint the remainder a light yellow or cream.

Make guide lines on the side of the cake by running a skewer or fine-pointed instrument in parallel lines about a quarter of an inch apart. Have the yellow royal icing about the same consistency as you would for flower-making, and place it in a bag with a number 22 basket weave tube attached.

Commencing at the top of the cake make a flat basket-weave line round the cake. Now place some of the brown-coloured royal icing in a bag with a number 1 writing tube attached and, at regular intervals over the horizontal lines, make vertical lines spaced about three-quarters of an inch apart.

Continue round the cake with vertical strokes of brown icing until the whole of the side is decorated. Make sure that the horizontal line covers the ends of the vertical strokes in the line above. These vertical lines of brown icing are always placed mid-way between those in the line above.

The Lid

Cut a circle of light cardboard 8 inches in diameter, then cut it through the centre to make two equal-sized pieces. Completely cover each piece with basket weave to match the sides of the cake. Trim the edge with dots piped with a number 1 writing tube.

Arrange the moulded roses and leaves round the edge of the cake and set the lid pieces on top. The roses, leaves and edge of the lid are secured to the cake with dabs of royal icing.

Complete the decoration with a bow of ribbon in the centre of the lid.

The lid is made in two pieces. Pipe the basket weave using a basket-weave or ribbon tube and a writing tube.

Daisy Cake

You will need:
>A rich fruit cake, butter weight ½ lb., baked
>in an 8-inch round cake tin (recipe on
>page 133)
>1½ lb. pink fondant icing
>Egg white for glazing
>One quantity of white royal icing
>About 4 dozen two-toned pink roses

Brush the surface of the cake with unbeaten egg white and cover with the pink fondant icing. Allow to become quite dry.

Using a pattern drawn on transparent paper, mark the top of the cake in 2-inch squares.

With white icing and a number 1 writing tube, pipe daisies as shown in the picture in the centre of each square. Using the same icing and tube, outline the squares, then circle the top edge of the cake with a series of lines similar to a tacking or basting stitch in sewing.

Mark the sides of the cake in nine equal parts and arrange a cluster of pink roses on each. Trim these with leaves of royal icing piped through a number 17 leaf tube. Change the tube and make the twisted tendrils with a number 00 tube.

Use the number 17 leaf tube and icing to make a border of leaves at the base of the cake.

Teenager's Dream Cake

Teenager's dream cake: make it in her favourite colours and set it on a silver board with a ruffle of pastel tulle.
Shown in colour on page 113

Pyramids of piped roses on the side balance the simple daisy design on the top of this cake.
Shown in colour on page 112

The daisies are piped directly onto the cake with a number 1 writing tube.

You will need:
> *A rich fruit cake, butter weight ½ lb., baked*
> *in an 8-inch heart-shaped cake tin (recipe*
> *on page 133)*
> *1 lb. almond paste*
> *Egg white and apricot jam for glazing*
> *1½ lb. fondant icing*
> *Moulded flowers and leaves*
> *Forget-me-nots (previously piped on paper)*
> *One quantity of royal icing*
> *Icing pincers*
> *Tulle for cake board*
> *Candles*
> *Food colourings*

Brush the cake with egg white or thinned and sieved apricot jam and cover with the almond icing. Allow to stand for several days.

Glaze the almond icing with egg white. Roll the fondant evenly and cover the entire surface, smoothing with the palms of the hands which have been dusted with sifted icing sugar. Trim the base and place the cake on a board lightly covered with paper.

Measure round the sides of the cake and divide evenly into scallops, each measuring about $1\frac{1}{2}$ inches; mark these lightly on the unset icing. Now, using $\frac{1}{2}$-inch icing pincers, make a scallop design just below the top edge of the cake. Leave until the fondant is quite firm. This will take at least twenty-four hours.

Completely cover the area below the scallop with the tiny forget-me-nots. Colour a quarter of the royal icing green and another quarter brown, and place alternate spoonfuls of these colours in a bag to which the small leaf tube has been attached. Pipe two-tone leaves between the flowers.

Using the remaining half quantity of royal icing tinted the same colour as the fondant, outline the scallop with a number 1 writing tube. Allow this to set.

Pipe, then flood, the figures for the teenager's age on waxed paper. When dry arrange them in an upright position on the cake, surrounding them with a ring of forget-me-nots and tiny leaves.

Make a spray with the moulded flowers and leaves on the top of the cake before setting it on a board covered with silver paper and trimmed with a ruffle of pastel pink bridal tulle.

Arrange the candles on the edge of the board, securing them to the board with royal icing or with candle wax, and adding a trimming, if you like, of forget-me-nots.

Spring Flowers for a 21st Birthday

You will need:
A rich fruit cake (three-quarters of the quantities in the $\frac{1}{2}$-lb. basic mixture—recipe on page 133) baked in a cake tin measuring 8 inches by $4\frac{1}{2}$ inches
1 lb. almond paste
Egg white and apricot jam for glazing
2 lb. fondant icing
A flooded key (see page 61)
Ribbon
Multicoloured piped flowers for the base
Roses and forget-me-nots for the top
One quantity of royal icing
Food colourings

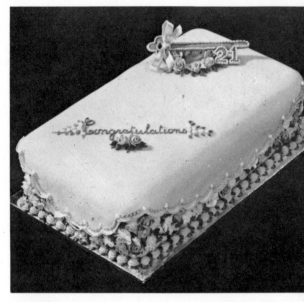

A scalloped overlay of blue fondant makes an effective trimming for this 21st birthday cake, which has masses of piped flowers and a flooded key as its main decoration.
Shown in colour on page 113

Level the top of the cake if necessary, brush with unbeaten egg white or thinned and sieved apricot jam, and cover with the almond icing. Leave for two or three days to become quite dry.

Brush with unbeaten egg white. Divide the fondant icing in two, but one portion, which is to be left white, should be a little larger than the other. Tint the smaller portion a pale blue by kneading a few drops of food colouring into it.

Cover the cake completely with the white fondant. When it has set, make an overlay with the blue fondant, scalloping the edge (using either a paper pattern or a small cutter). Allow the icing to dry overnight.

With pastel blue royal icing outline the scallops, using a fine writing tube. Trim the edge of each scallop with dots of the same icing and decorate with tiny forget-me-nots.

Over the white fondant which is not covered with the blue overlay, arrange masses of multi-coloured flowers and pipe two-toned green leaves.

Colour some of the royal icing pale pink and pipe a shell border round the base. When the icing has set, pipe a two-toned green leaf in between each shell.

The Key

To make the key, follow the picture guide and the detailed instructions.

Tie a bow of narrow ribbon on the end of the flooded key and attach it to one corner of the cake with royal icing. Pack a pad of cotton wool lightly at the back of the key to hold it in position until the icing dries, then remove the cotton wool.

Add a circle of pink roses and leaves round the key, and complete the decorations by writing "Congratulations" in brown royal icing through a number 00 tube and trimming with roses, forget-me-nots and leaves.

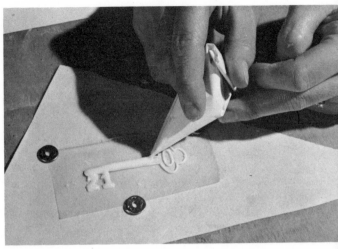

Step 2: Thin down some royal icing with cold water or lemon juice. With a thicker writing tube or a paper funnel fill in or flood the outline, easing the icing into the curves with a small watercolour brush. Allow to dry overnight.

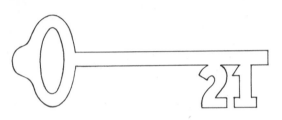

The key outline for flooding. Step 1: Trace the key shape on a piece of paper, cover with waxed paper and attach securely to a board, waxed side up. Outline the shape of the key with royal icing through a fine writing tube and allow the icing to become partly dry.

Step 3: To remove the key from the paper, take out the pin tacks, move the paper to the edge of the table, and gently ease it from the back of the iced key. The key is very fragile and needs careful handling. A dab of icing on the back holds it to the cake.

61

Two-tier 21st Birthday Cake

Here is another idea for using flooded keys and moulded roses on a 21st birthday cake. You will need a 1¼-lb. butter-weight mixture (2½ times the quantities given in the basic ½-lb. mixture on page 133). The bottom tier uses the double quantity baked in a 10-inch square cake tin, while the top tier uses the remaining half quantity (i.e., ¼ lb. butter weight) and is baked in a 6-inch square cake tin, then placed on top without the aid of pillars.

Each cake is covered separately. The shell pattern at the base of the top tier covers the join.

A two-tier 21st birthday cake featuring flooded keys and moulded roses
Shown in colour on page 114

Key-shaped 21st Birthday Cake

A key-shaped cake makes an effective table centrepiece for a coming-of-age party. All you need do to make it suitable for either a boy or a girl is to change the character of the icing and decoration. A floral, frilly design is most suitable for the girl's cake; marzipan moulded into miniature fruit shapes with the addition of some piped bunches of grapes is one idea for a feature on a boy's cake.

Use a double quantity of the basic ½-lb. rich fruit mixture (recipe on page 133), baking it in three tins: you need a 7-inch or 8-inch ring tin and two bar tins each 10 by 3 by 2 inches. Half the mixture is baked in the ring tin and the remainder divided equally between the two bar tins.

To shape the cakes, take a pastry cutter the same size as the width of the bar tin and cut a piece from one of the bar cakes to fit the curve of the ring cake. This makes the main part of the key. The second bar cake is used to make the two "bits", as they are called (in other words the two right-angled parts on the key): it is cut in half, then one of the halves is cut in two. The half piece makes the upper right-angled part of the key and one of the quarter pieces makes the lower right-angled part (you'll have the second quarter left over).

For the icing and decoration you will need:

For either cake
{
2 lb. almond paste
2½ to 3 lb. fondant icing
Egg white and apricot jam for
  glazing
}

Boy's cake
{
Miniature fruits moulded from al-
  mond paste and painted with food
  colourings
One quantity of royal icing
21 candles in a colour to suit a boy
}

Girl's cake
{
Floribunda roses and buds moulded
  in fondant icing
Filigree lace edging made in royal
  icing
One quantity of royal icing
Ribbon
21 candles in a colour to suit a girl
}

21st birthday key cake for a boy. Keep the decorations simple: moulded marzipan fruits and a piped grape design trim this cake.
Shown in colour on page 114

Shaping the cakes. Cut a piece from the end of one of the bar cakes, and use the second bar cake to make the key "bits".

For the boy's cake, first make the miniature fruits by moulding pieces of almond paste into the various shapes. Put these aside for several days to become quite dry. Paint with food colourings and leave to dry. Use cloves for the stems and the "blossom" end of the fruits.

Covering Either Cake

Trim off any rough pieces from the surface and brush with either unbeaten egg white or thinned and sieved apricot jam.

Place the long bar cake with the curved section cut from the edge adjoining the ring cake.

Take half the almond paste and roll it into an oblong large enough to cover the two cakes. Dust the hands with sifted icing sugar and mould the paste into the inner ring of the cake, also smoothing it over the bar cake. Trim all edges.

Use the remainder of the paste to cover the two quarters cut for the right-angled pieces on the key. Trim the base of these two pieces and let them stand for two or three days.

Brush the almond covering lightly with unbeaten egg white, then roll out the fondant paste a little thicker than the almond layer and use the same method to cover the cakes with it.

While the fondant icing is still soft transfer the cake to a covered board, brush lightly with egg white where the bits will join and press the two key bits into position. Leave until the fondant is dry before decorating.

21st birthday key cake for a girl: pretty pink moulded roses and a lace edging add the feminine touch.
Shown in colour on page 115

Decorating the Boy's Cake

Have the royal icing a little firmer than one would use for a border design, and select a number 1 writing tube. The grapes are piped directly onto the cake. First make a foundation in the shape of a rough triangle: this is done by running the tube backwards and forwards on the cake.

With the tube in a slanting position, and shaping the bunch of grapes from the wide or stem end to the single grape, press, releasing the icing in bursts, then lower the tube and tuck the end under the row just piped. Continue piping as described, each row of grapes being made without lifting the tube: each succeeding row is begun under the one before it, and you tuck the end of the tube under each time. Graduate the number of grapes in each row, ending with a single grape, and as you pipe give the bunch a slight twist rather than making the rows straight, so as to produce a more natural appearance.

A few fine tendrils made with a number 00 tube are now added to each bunch. Touch the cake lightly with the tip of the tube, then twist and curl the icing as it comes from the tube.

Add small leaves with the same icing through a number 17 leaf tube.

This grape design is piped in a scallop round the ring and the two small cakes. It is used, too, where the two small or right-angled pieces of cake are attached.

Using a number 8 star tube make a shell edge on the border of the cake. Attach the small pieces of fruit in groups of three on the ring cake, securing them with a little royal icing and adding a few leaves of royal icing.

Write the boy's name on the bar of the cake with a fine writing tube.

Cover a piece of board with the same silver or gold paper as was used for the board on which the main cake is placed, and attach the 21 candles with royal icing. Or have an extra candle, light it, and as the wax drips onto the board set the candles in position.

Decorating the Girl's Cake

Make up a number of floribunda roses (see page 20) from the fondant icing you are using to cover the cake, including a few buds (there should be sufficient fondant left over). Let these roses and buds set and become quite dry. With well-worked royal icing make the lace edge for the cake: for

The grapes: use a number 1 writing tube for the raised grape edging on the boy's 21st birthday cake.

The lace edge for the girl's cake (actual size)

this you need a number 00 writing tube to trace the outline in icing onto the waxed paper. A fine watercolour brush will help you ease the icing into the pattern. Leave until thoroughly dry before removing from the paper.

Cover the cake with the almond and fondant paste in the same way as described for the boy's cake. Place it on a covered board with two right-angled pieces of the key in position.

Arrange a circle of the floribunda roses round the centre of the ring cake. Add leaves of royal icing through a small leaf tube.

Make the lacework the day before it is to be used on the cake. To attach it, take a number 1 writing tube and some royal icing and pipe small dots round the edge of the cake (don't pipe all the dots at once—but pipe a few and attach a small section of lacework at a time, otherwise the dots will dry too soon). You carefully lift the lace pattern in sections from the paper and place them in position on the piped icing dots. When all the lacework is dry, pipe a row of tiny dots above each lace motif, using the same coloured royal icing.

Arrange the candles as for the young man's cake, and trim the cake with a bow of satin ribbon the same colour as the covering icing.

Another Key-shaped
21st Birthday Cake

Here is a variation of the key-shaped cake, made with the same quantity of rich fruit mixture. This time the larger cake is made in an 8-inch round cake tin instead of a ring tin, and you also need the two smaller cake tins to make the key, as in the cake just described. The same amount of almond and fondant icing is needed; only the decorations are different.

Make a circle of piped or moulded flowers and leaves on the round cake. Measure the outside of the cake and mark it evenly into one-inch divisions. Using a paper icing bag or a number 0 icing tube, string scallop a pattern round the cake. Cut the bar cakes as before and repeat the string scallop pattern on the long bar cake and on the two "bits" or right-angled parts of the key cakes. Fill in the join where the two smaller cakes meet the larger bar cake with a row of royal icing dots. Shell edge the base.

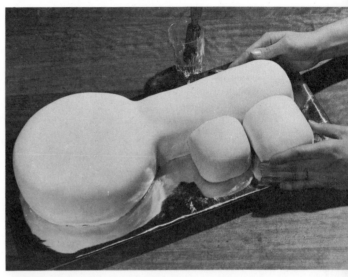

The key assembled and covered

Another key-shaped cake for a 21st birthday. A round tin is used to bake the main cake this time.

Piping the scallop. When the ring of moulded roses has been placed on top of the main cake, trim the edges with a string scallop.

65

Silver Keys and Shaded Roses for a 21st Birthday

Trimmed with shaded roses and silver keys, this cake is suitable for a boy's or a girl's 21st birthday.
Shown in colour on page 115

Silver keys and subtly tinted roses, becoming lighter in shade towards the tips, make this design for a 21st birthday cake. You will need:

A rich fruit cake, ½ lb. butter weight, baked in an 8-inch round cake tin (recipe on page 133)
1 lb. almond paste
Egg white and apricot jam for glazing
1½ lb. fondant icing
Piped roses
6 flooded keys (see page 61)
One quantity of royal icing
Food colourings
Silver colouring powder
Banana oil

Level the cake, brush with unbeaten egg white or thinned and sieved apricot jam and then cover with the rolled almond paste. Trim the base and leave for several days before brushing with unbeaten egg white and covering with the fondant icing.

Make a circle of the piped roses, adding a cluster at the top and base of the circle. Add a trimming of leaves.

Mix silver powder with banana oil and paint the keys after the icing has set, using a fine watercolour brush. Let them dry. (If silver powder is not available, flood the keys with an icing to match the deepest colour in the roses.) Remember that this silver powder is not edible, and is only used on decorations that can be removed before the cake is cut.

Set one silver flooded key inside the circle of roses on the top of the cake, and space the remaining five at equal distances round the side of the cake, attaching them with a little royal icing.

Write a greeting in pink, blue or lemon royal icing with number 00 tube, and trim the base with flat stars, using the same icing through a number 8 star tube.

Miniature Fruits on a 21st Birthday Cake

You will need:

A rich fruit cake mixture, butter weight ½ lb., baked in an 8-inch round cake tin (recipe on page 133)
1 lb. almond paste
Egg white and apricot jam for glazing
1½ lb. fondant icing
A double quantity of royal icing
Miniature fruits moulded from almond paste
A flooded key (see page 61)
Food colourings

Lightly brush the cake with unbeaten egg white or thinned and sieved apricot jam. Knead the almond paste until it is easily rolled, roll thinly and cover the cake. Reserve the pieces trimmed from the base: these will be moulded into miniature fruits to decorate the cake. Mould the fruits the day before they are to be used, painting them with vegetable colourings.

Colour the fondant icing a pale blue and roll it a little smaller than the cake. Brush the almond covering with unbeaten egg white, then cover with the fondant, easing down with the palms of the hands which have been dipped in sifted icing sugar. Trim the base. Leave until the following day before decorating.

Cut a 6½-inch circle of greaseproof paper and mark it into eight scallops. Place on top of the cake, prick out the scallops and, using pale blue royal icing through a number 00 writing tube, pipe their outline.

Using the same tube and icing, stipple the sides and top of the cake, leaving the 6½-inch centre circle uncovered.

Arrange clusters of the moulded almond paste fruits at the point of each scallop, attaching them with dabs of royal icing.

Use a number 8 star tube to pipe a shell border at the base of the cake.

Place the key a little higher than the centre of the cake. To keep the key upright, lightly pack small balls of cotton wool behind it until the icing dries.

On waxed paper flood the letters to make the name of the birthday boy. When dry attach them to the cake with royal icing.

Mark the eight scallops on top of the cake, and fill in the sides with this simple but effective stippling design.

Engagement Cake

A fruit cake baked in two heart-shaped cake tins, then joined with icing, makes this attractive flower-decorated engagement cake. You will need:

> *A rich fruit cake, butter weight 1 lb., divided and baked in two heart-shaped cake tins (double the quantities in the ½-lb. butter-weight recipe on page 133)*
> *2½ lb. almond paste*
> *3 lb. fondant icing*
> *Egg white and apricot jam for glazing*
> *Moulded roses, single azaleas and leaves*
> *One quantity of royal icing*
> *A tulle ruffle*

Place the two cakes side by side on a board and, using the side of one of the heart-shaped tins as your guide, mark out a section of one cake in which to fit the side of the other. Brush with thinned and sieved apricot jam and fit the two cakes snugly together.

Brush with more thinned jam or with unbeaten egg white, then roll the almond paste evenly and cover the cakes. Leave until the icing is dry, then cover in the same way with the fondant, glazing first with unbeaten egg white (not jam this time).

Leave until the fondant icing is quite dry before decorating. To get away from the more formal pipework, especially on a floral cake, borders or edges of relief work, which use a combination

Almond paste was moulded into miniature fruits to trim this 21st birthday cake.
Shown in colour on page 115

of brush and icing tube work, are suggested.

Here are three examples of relief work. We have used the first on the engagement cake, as illustrated. While this is mostly freehand, it is a good idea to mark the width and depth of the scallop and plan the spacing before commencing.

For the top border use a small leaf tube or cut a paper cone. Pipe four feather-like elongated leaf shapes directly onto the cake. Now take a fine watercolour brush and draw the tip through the icing, tapering the ends and at the same time giving a sculptured look to the icing. With a very small paper cone cut as a leaf tube, make five tiny leaves between the larger elongated ones. Continue in the same way, having five small leaves in between each pair of the larger sculptured leaves.

For the floral festoon, also illustrated, mark the scallops on the cake; then, with the same tiny leaf tube or paper cone, pipe miniature leaves, graduating them in size from the tip to the drop of the scallop. On the curve of each scallop make little swirls of icing through the same tube, and before it has set take a watercolour brush and model the icing to form small roses.

For the third pattern simply pipe small shapes with a leaf tube in a scallop design, then run the tip of a watercolour brush through the centre of each to deepen the vein.

Allow the relief border to dry before decorating with the moulded flowers. Arrange the sprays on the cake. Add moulded leaves which have been painted with green and brown icing, and set the two cakes on a prepared board complete with a ruffle of tulle.

If liked, the names of the engaged couple may be piped directly onto the cake.

Trim the board with posies of the same flowers as you have chosen for the top of the cakes.

A rich fruit cake mixture was baked in two heart-shaped tins for this pretty engagement cake. Shown in colour on page 116

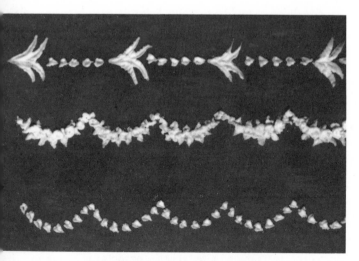

Three examples of relief borders

A close-up of the spray of moulded flowers decorating the twin-heart engagement cake

Simple Elegance
for a Wedding Cake

This single-tier wedding cake with a simple design of stippling and moulded roses is also suitable for a golden wedding anniversary. The colour is a matter of personal taste. You will need:

> *A wedding cake, butter weight 1 lb., baked in a 10-inch round cake tin (recipe on page 133)*
> *2 lb. almond paste*
> *Egg white and apricot jam for glazing*
> *2 lb. fondant icing*
> *¼ yard bridal tulle*
> *Piped roses*
> *One quantity of royal icing*

If necessary level off the surface of the cake and brush away any loose crumbs. Glaze with unbeaten egg white or thinned and sieved apricot jam. Knead then roll the almond paste to an even thickness and cover the cake. Let it stand for two or three days.

Brush with unbeaten egg white and cover smoothly with the rolled fondant icing. Trim the base of the cake and allow it to become set and dry.

Prepare a cake board at least 2 inches larger in diameter than the cake, covering it with gold or

Moulded roses and a stippled design for a simple wedding cake
Shown in colour on page 117

The dotted border is made with a number 2 writing tube, and piped roses are placed at intervals round the cake.

silver paper and pinning or attaching to it with adhesive tape or paper a frill of bridal tulle.

Mark a six-inch circle in the centre of the cake. Measure round the cake and mark into twenty even sections. Draw a scallop pattern (see page 3) and prick the outline onto the cake, or draw it lightly with a fine skewer.

Using a fine writing tube, preferably number 00, stipple in the area between the centre circle on the top of the cake and the scallops on the side. Dot the edge of the scallops on the side of the cake, and inside the circle on the cake top.

Arrange five sprays of two-tone piped roses on the top, securing them with a little royal icing, and add light-green leaves and tendrils in royal icing the same colour as the fondant, piping them with a number 00 tube.

Place the cake on the prepared board. Using a number 2 writing tube make large dots of the same coloured icing as the fondant at the base of the cake, then add, at the point below the curve of each scallop on the side of the cake, a rose and one or two piped leaves in the same colouring.

69

Two-tier Heart-shaped Wedding Cake

Two heart-shaped tiers make up this pretty cake which features moulded roses as its main decoration.

For a double-tiered cake baked in the standard round 10-inch and 6-inch tins respectively it is usual to have a mixture of 1¼ lb. butter weight, but because of the slightly larger size and the irregular shape of the tins used for this cake it is recommended that the quantity be increased to a 1½-lb. butter-weight mixture (see Wedding Cake recipe on page 133). As well you will need:

3 lb. almond paste
3 lb. fondant icing
Egg white or apricot jam for glazing
About 10 moulded roses for each of the 3 sprays on the bottom tier, plus a few buds; and about 5 moulded roses plus buds for each of the 3 sprays on the top tier
One quantity of royal icing for piping
3 glass pillars and 3 wooden skewers
Flooded birds (see page 81)
A ruffle of tulle

Sprays of moulded roses with piped leaves and bluebirds decorate this pretty heart-shaped wedding cake.

Prepare the cake in the usual way by brushing with thinned and sieved apricot jam before covering with the almond paste. Allow to stand for several days, then brush with unbeaten egg white and cover with the fondant. Trim the base and allow to become quite dry before decorating.

Set the cake neatly on the gold or silver paper covered board with its tulle ruffle. Mark the position of the sprays on both the top and bottom tiers. Attach the roses with a little royal icing and add rose leaves and stems with royal icing.

Measure between the sprays on the side of each cake and mark at one-inch intervals, then with a number 00 writing tube pipe string scallops between the sprays, using the inch marks as a guide.

With a number 0 writing tube pipe string scallops between the sprays of moulded roses for the border design.

Place the pillars in position. Run the wooden skewers down through the bottom cake tier until the tip of the skewer touches the board. Place the glass pillars over the wooden skewers and mark the skewers level with the tops of the pillars. Remove skewers and pillars and cut the surplus from the wooden skewers. Cover the portion of each skewer that will show through the glass pillars with silver or gold paper.

Place the skewers and pillars in position.

Make the flooded birds and when they are perfectly dry place them between the rose sprays on both the top and bottom tiers. Pipe a bow in pale blue or white royal icing through a fine writing tube.

Complete by piping a shell border in royal icing at the base of each cake.

A posy of fresh flowers is suggested as a top decoration.

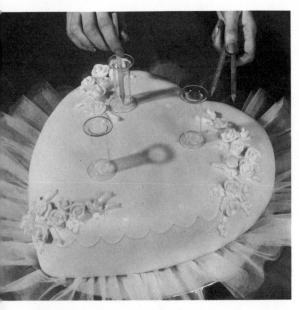

Placing the skewers inside the glass pillars. Mark the positions of the three pillars accurately before securing to the cake.

Two-tier Pink Rose Wedding Cake

You will need:

> A 1½-lb. wedding cake mixture baked in three
>   7½-inch square cake tins (see page 135)
> 3 lb. almond paste
> 3 lb. pink fondant icing for covering
> ½ lb. extra pink fondant icing for modelling
>   4 roses and about 3 dozen leaves
> Egg white and apricot jam for glazing
> Pink ribbon
> Pink tulle
> 3 covered boards 8½ inches in diameter
> 4 pink pillars and 4 wooden skewers
> One quantity of pink royal icing

It is almost certain that you will have to make up the cake mixture in two batches, because you will not be able to fit the three cakes in the oven at the one time. You could double the ½-lb.

In this unusual design for a wedding cake, each tier is decorated with outlined roses.
Shown in colour on page 116

butter-weight mixture (see page 134) and bake two of the cakes at the same time, then make up the single mixture for the third cake.

Trim the surface of each cake if necessary and brush away any loose crumbs. Glaze with unbeaten egg white or some thinned and sieved apricot jam and then cover with the rolled almond paste.

After the almond paste has been on the cake for a week, brush the surface with unbeaten egg white and cover with the fondant icing. Smooth with the hands which have been dusted with sifted icing sugar, and trim the base with a sharp knife.

The cake that is to form the top tier will require eight outlined roses. The remaining two cakes will only need six, because the pillars will take up the rest of the space on top of the cake.

On greaseproof or waxed paper trace the rose pattern. Place the tracing lightly on the cake and mark the outline of each rose with a pin, at even intervals round the cake. Commencing each rose about two-thirds of the distance from the base of the cake, with a number 00 writing tube and pink royal icing follow the outlines of the rose, leaves, and stem. Allow this icing to set.

Make four moulded roses and about three dozen leaves from pale pink fondant (see method on page 99, Golden Wedding Cake).

Cut the pink tulle into strips each 2 inches wide (you'll need a length three times the circumference of the cake). Gather with a running thread

71

The rose outline, actual size

and attach to the covered cake board with drawing pins. Make a tulle frill for each cake.

Tie a narrow band of pink ribbon round each cake, then, using a star tube (number 5), make a scroll design between the ribbon and the base of the cake.

Place the pillars in position and run a wooden skewer down the centre of each, marking each skewer at the top of the pillar. Lift them out of the cake, cut off the surplus, and replace them. These wooden skewers take the weight of the cake and prevent the pillars sinking into the icing.

Attach the roses and leaves to the top of the cakes, securing them with a little royal icing. Place the top tier in position and the cake is completed.

Two-tier Rose Garland Wedding Cake

You will need:

A wedding cake, $1\frac{1}{4}$ lb. butter weight, baked in two round cake tins, one 10 inches in diameter and the other 6 inches (see page 135)
3 lb. almond paste
3 lb. fondant icing
Egg white and apricot jam for glazing
Several dozen piped roses
1 yard white bridal tulle
One quantity of royal icing
Milliner's wire
Small bows of satin ribbon about $\frac{1}{4}$ inch wide
4 pillars

To decorate, first make the cakes level on top if necessary. Brush away any loose crumbs, glaze the surface with unbeaten egg white or thinned and sieved apricot jam and cover with almond paste, smoothing with the palms of the hands which have been dusted with icing sugar. Trim the base. Leave for a week, then brush with unbeaten egg white and cover with fondant icing. Leave another two or three days before decorating.

Dozens of roses piped from royal icing are the featured decoration on this cake. Make the roses (page 17) and allow them to become quite dry and set.

Now take a strip of paper 3 inches wide and trim it to the outside measurement of the large cake. Divide it evenly into 9 sections and cut each into a scallop (see illustration). Mark the scallops on to the cake with a fine skewer, then attach the roses to the cake with a little royal icing, following the line of the scallop and massing the roses to fill in the space to the base of the cake.

Using white royal icing through a number 17 leaf tube, pipe leaves between the roses, and with a number 1 writing tube pipe in the small stems and tendrils.

Repeat the same pattern on the top tier of the cake, this time with six scallops instead of nine.

Have a cake board about 14 inches in diameter and cover it with gold or silver paper. Cut a double strip of bridal tulle about 4 inches wide and run a gathering thread on one side. Gather it up to make a ruffle and attach it to the board with drawing pins, or with adhesive tape or paper.

Centre the bottom tier of the cake on the prepared board.

Arrange four pillars on top of the cake. Run a skewer down the centre of each and trim it off at the top of the pillar.

Complete the decorations with a posy of piped roses set in a tulle ruffle.

The wired roses. Pipe each sugar rose on one end of a piece of milliner's wire instead of on a skewer or matchstick. Leave until dry. Gather up a bunch of these wired roses and set them in the ruffle of tulle. Trim the ends of the wire, making them even, and press into the top of the cake.

Add a tiny bow of white satin ribbon at the base of each scallop on both the top and bottom tier.

Masses of small piped roses with piped leaves of royal icing and bows of satin ribbon form an effective decoration on this double-tiered wedding cake.

Cut a strip of paper 3 inches wide and trim it to the outside measurement of the large cake. Divide it into nine equal-sized scallops and mark their outline on the cake with a skewer.

73

Two-tier Floribunda Rose Wedding Cake

The cake is made from the same wedding cake mixture as the Rose Garland Cake. For icing and decoration you will need:

    3 lb. almond paste
    3 lb. fondant icing
    Egg white and apricot jam for glazing
    5 pillars and 5 skewers
    Floribunda roses and buds moulded from
      fondant
    Lacework
    Flooded bells
    Bridal tulle

A spray of fresh white flowers adds a charming touch to a rose-decorated wedding cake.

Follow the instructions for making and covering the cakes as given for the Rose Garland Wedding Cake. Only the type of decoration and the number of pillars will differ.

The floribunda roses are moulded from the same fondant as was used for covering the cake (there should be enough left over). Make them according to the instructions given on page 20, graduating them in size and allowing three sprays for the bottom tier, but as soon as you have completed one rose, take a pair of tweezers, pluck out the centre, and insert small flower stamens (the type used for French-flower making). These will set in place as the icing dries.

The roses for this cake are made in the same way as formal roses, but before the icing sets pull out the centre with tweezers and insert some milliner's wire stamens with a little royal icing.

For the rosebuds, roll small pieces of fondant as you would for the centre of the moulded rose, but do not add any outside petals.

The bells and the bow are made in two separate operations.

First measure the outside of the cake and mark the position of the bells and the sprays. On the bottom tier there will be two sets of bow and bells between each spray of roses. For the top tier you will need five sets of bow and bells but no rose sprays.

Using the pattern given on page 75, make a tracing of the bow on waxed paper and prick the outline onto the cake with a pin. Outline it with royal icing through a number 00 tube and, when it has set, flood in the outline with the same royal icing thinned down with a little water or lemon juice. Use a fine watercolour brush to smooth the flooded icing.

Meanwhile, on waxed paper, trace, then flood in the twin bell outline and, when set, cover one bell completely with dots of royal icing and outline the opening of the other bell with a fine writing tube.

For the lace scallop, outline pattern with royal icing through a fine tube and, when it has dried, match it up in pairs to attach it to the cake.

Set the bottom tier on a covered board which has had a ruffle of tulle attached to it. Attach the rose sprays with royal icing and add leaves of royal icing through a number 17 leaf tube.

Pipe a shell border round the base of the cake and set the pillars in position, running a skewer down the centre of each to keep it steady and cutting the top of the skewer level with the top of the pillar.

Decorate the top of the cake with a spray of fresh white flowers such as white azaleas or gardenias.

The pattern for the bow and bells

The lace pattern for the floribunda rose cake

Two-tier Rose Wedding Cake

Choose your own colour scheme for this attractive rose-patterned wedding cake but keep to pastel colours and make the roses small.

Use the same sized tins and the same quantity of wedding cake mixture, almond paste and fondant icing as for the Floribunda Rose Cake. Four pillars are sufficient for this cake, and in addition to about 108 piped roses you need sculptured bluebirds and tiny forget-me-nots.

Follow the instructions for making and covering the cakes as given for the Rose Garland Wedding Cake.

When ready to decorate, measure round each cake and mark into seven divisions for the bottom tier and five for the top tier, so that the roses can be placed at equal distances apart. At each marking attach six roses to make an oval shape. Join these ovals of roses with festoons of roses and leaves, using three blooms between

75

each oval. Add leaves and tendrils of royal icing, with tube number 17 for the leaves and number 00 for the tendrils.

Between each oval of roses, in the centre, attach tiny forget-me-nots in a circle. Pipe bluebirds (brushing to give a sculptured effect), each holding in its beak a bow of blue ribbon made with a fine writing tube.

Set the cake on a covered board which has had a ruffle of tulle attached to it. Place the pillars in position, running a skewer down the centre of each to keep it firmly in place. Make scallops of forget-me-nots between the pillars.

With a number 8 star tube shell edge both cakes, and attach a bouquet of fresh flowers to the top tier.

Pipe a shell border at the base of the cake with a number 8 star tube.

For a sculptured effect, lightly brush the bluebirds after they have been flooded.

When the decorations have been completed on the bottom tier, place it on a covered board and set the pillars in position.

Two-tier Blossom and Bell Wedding Cake

This light and pretty design combines the delicacy of sugar lacework with small piped flowers. It carries as a top piece a sugar bell trimmed with the same piped flowers as are used on the cake. As it is a two-tiered cake you'll require the same ingredients and quantities as for the Rose Garland Wedding Cake. It is covered with almond icing and fondant in the same way. For the decorations you will need:

> 20 piped single blossoms
> 30 piped half blossoms
> 30 piped flower buds
> Extra piped flowers for trimming the bell
> Fondant icing for the bell shape
> One quantity of royal icing
> At least 180 lace motifs
> ¼ yard bridal tulle
> A small plastic or sugar bell shape
> Narrow white satin ribbon

On waxed paper, with royal icing and a number 20 petal tube, make the single blossoms, half blossoms and buds for the scallop design on the cake.

Sugar lacework with small piped flowers and a decorated sugar bell adorn this charming blossom and bell wedding cake.

The lace motifs are piped on waxed paper and allowed to dry before being placed in pairs on the iced cake.

The Lace Motifs

The pieces of lace are to be matched in pairs on the cake, so they must be uniform in size. The only way to be sure is to draw the small designs on a piece of thick white paper in heavy pencil. Place this on a board and cover it with a sheet of waxed paper. Insert drawing pins to keep both sheets of paper in place. With well-worked royal icing and a number 00 writing tube outline the design, using the tip of a fine watercolour brush to adjust any irregularities, and leave until quite dry.

When you have completed the rows of lace on the first piece of waxed paper lift the paper and replace it with another piece. Continue until you have enough to put together in pairs and scatter over the surface of the cake. It will take about 60 pairs for the top tier and double that number for the bottom.

These little shapes are extremely fragile and should be handled carefully. To remove them from the paper, use a razor blade or your finger nail. It is always wise to make more than you need because the breakage rate is usually high.

Scallop Pattern for the Blossom

Measure round the larger cake and mark into twelve even sections, then the smaller cake and mark into eight sections. You will need twelve scallops for the bottom tier and eight for the top—mark these on each cake with a pin or a fine skewer. Attach the blossoms with a little royal icing and trim with leaves made with a number 17 leaf tube. On the points of the scallops decorate with dots of royal icing with a number 1 writing tube.

Attach the lace motifs to the cake in pairs, securing them with tiny dots of royal icing.

Place the cakes on the prepared boards—the one for the top tier has a narrow ruffle of tulle round it.

The Wedding Bell

Roll some of the covering fondant very thinly. Take a small plastic bell shape (these are available from chain stores) and cover it completely with the icing. Trim the edges and leave till dry. Now carefully loosen the bell and remove it from the icing. You should have a perfectly moulded bell shape. Trim it with some of the same single blossoms that were used on the cake.

(If you are unable to buy a plastic bell shape the size you require, buy a sugar paste bell from a shop that stocks cake decorating equipment and trim it with piped blossoms.)

Attach the decorated bell to the cake—its streamers of satin ribbon will trail over to one side.

To make the bell, use fondant thinly rolled and moulded round a plastic bell shape. Trim the edges and allow the bell to dry before decorating it.

A close-up of the bell, which like the cake is trimmed with single blossoms.

78

Three-tier Bell and Lace Wedding Cake

Flooded bells, lacework, and moulded roses on a dainty three-tier wedding cake

Here is a wedding cake decorated with moulded roses, flooded bells and sugar lacework, and trimmed with ribbon and tulle. It would be equally attractive iced in white or a pastel pink. You will need:

A wedding cake, 1¾ lb. butter weight, baked in three square tins 10 inches, 8 inches and 6 inches in diameter (see page 135)
4 lb. almond icing
Egg white and apricot jam for glazing
5½ lb. fondant icing
One quantity of royal icing
Moulded roses and buds, about 60 in all
28 sets of flooded bells (see page 79)
32 tiny bows of satin ribbon
Sugar lacework

Patterns for the lacework

Bridal tulle
8 pillars and 8 wooden skewers

Trim each cake if necessary, brush away any loose crumbs, and glaze with thinned and sieved apricot jam. Cover with almond icing, smoothing with the hands which have been dusted with sifted icing sugar. Trim the base of each and leave to stand for several days. Brush with un-beaten egg white and cover with fondant, trim-ming the bases and allowing the icing to become quite set before decorating.

Choose one of the lace patterns shown here. Make sure you have extra pieces in case of breakage. Pipe on to waxed paper and leave till quite dry.

Mould the roses and the buds from some of the fondant.

Trace the outline of the bells, then follow the directions for flooding on page 80. To give a rounded effect to each bell, make a second flooding of icing on the top.

The clappers are piped on after the flooded icing has dried, as are the dots.

Make sure you leave these flooded bells at least twenty-four hours before attempting to remove them from the paper.

Mark the position of the bells, and prick with a pin where the lacework will be placed. Mark the position of the pillars.

Set each tier, when the covering icing is quite dry, on covered boards which have tulle ruffles. The ruffles on the second and top tier should only protrude about half an inch from the edge of the board. The bottom ruffle should be about 3 or 4 inches wide.

Add the trimmings in this order: first the flowers, attaching them with a little royal icing, then the piped leaves through a number 17 leaf tube, and fine tendrils through a number 00 tube or a fine paper cone. Add the bells, then, using a large star tube, shell edge the bottom of the cake where it meets the tulle. The icing will be easier to pipe if you hold the tulle flat with the left hand while you pipe with the right.

To hold the scalloped lace make small dots of royal icing in the pattern the lace will take, then place it in position. Try to have the lace standing out a little from the side of the cake.

Lastly add the ribbon bows, fixing them to the cake with tiny dabs of royal icing.

A pretty finish for the top of this cake is a posy matching either the bride's or the bridesmaid's bouquet.

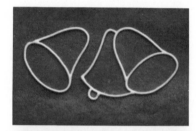

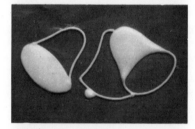

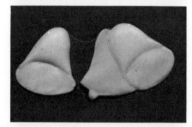

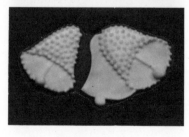

Stages in making the flooded bells (actual size)

Flooded Bells

An idea for a wedding or an anniversary cake decoration is flooded bells. The same technique as for a flooded key is used. Draw or trace a bell shape on waxed paper. Using royal icing through a fine writing tube, outline the shape. Now thin down some of the royal icing with water or lemon juice and flood in the outline.

To give a rounded effect to the bell make a thicker flooding of icing at the top of the bell, or flood it a second time, making sure the first flooding is perfectly dry before adding the second layer.

The clapper for the bell is piped on after the flooding icing has dried, as are the dots. Both are made with royal icing through a fine writing tube.

Leave each bell when completed for at least twenty-four hours before removing from the waxed paper.

Take out the pin tack holding the waxed paper to the board, move the paper containing the bell to the edge of the table, then carefully draw the paper away from the bell.

Attach each bell to the cake by placing a small dab of royal icing on the back and pressing the bell gently into position.

Three-tier Heart-shaped Wedding Cake

A difference in the shape of the tins can add interest to a wedding cake, and heart-shaped tins are always popular. As they are slightly larger than the round or square tins so often used for a three-tier wedding cake, it is recommended that the ingredients include 2 lb. butter and correspondingly larger quantities of the other ingredients. You will need:

3 heart-shaped wedding cakes baked in 12-inch, 8-inch and 6-inch tins (see page 135)
4 lb. almond paste
Egg white or apricot jam for glazing
5 lb. fondant icing
One quantity of modelling paste for the roses (see page 9)

Sprays of moulded single roses, with tulle leaves and a minimum of pipework, make up the decorations on a heart-shaped wedding cake. Shown in colour on page 118

Flower stamens
A double quantity of royal icing
Piped bluebirds
½ yard pastel pink bridal tulle
Fresh flowers and ribbon for the top of the cake
8 pillars and 8 wooden skewers

Prepare the surface of each cake, brushing away any crumbs after levelling the top of the cakes if necessary. Glaze lightly with unbeaten egg white or thinned and sieved apricot jam.

Knead the almond paste, using a little sifted icing sugar, and divide it into three, having one portion larger for the bottom tier.

For each cake dust the rolling pin lightly with sifted icing sugar and roll the paste slightly smaller than the overall area of the top and sides of the cake. Lift carefully onto the cake, then smooth with the hands which have been dusted with icing sugar. Trim the surplus almond paste from the base. Allow the cakes to stand for one week. Cover each with the fondant, using the same method as for the almond paste but brushing with unbeaten egg white—not jam in this case.

Make up the modelling fondant and work it well with the fingers until pliable. Break off six small pieces and mould each into a rose petal shape. See instructions on page 20.

Mould six small pieces of the fondant for each rose. With a dab of royal icing in the centre of each, attach stamens of milliner's wire.

Graduate the size of the blossoms. You'll need five for a spray on the bottom tier; four on the middle tier; and three on the top tier. A few buds will add interest to the decoration, and a few blossoms for the base and centre top of the bottom tier and the side of the middle tier.

The leaves are made from pieces of tulle. Cut the tulle into leaf shapes, then, using a fine writing tube and pale pink royal icing, pipe in the veins and outline. Leave these to dry over the handle of a wooden spoon to give them a more interesting shape.

Six piped bluebirds are made from pale blue royal icing. Trace the outline of the bird on paper, cover it with waxed paper and trace the outline in pale blue royal icing through a number 00 tube. Thin down the remainder of the blue icing and flood the outline, using a fine water-colour brush to ease the icing into the wing-tips and beak. Leave to dry until the following day.

Dot the head of each bird with a speck of black colouring to represent the eye.

If you are more experienced in pipework, you may pipe the birds directly onto the cake.

Mark the position of the pillars on the bottom and middle tiers. Arrange the flower sprays on each cake, attaching the flowers with a little royal icing. Do not add the leaves at this stage.

Tulle leaves add a delicate touch to the flower sprays. Outline them with royal icing through a fine writing tube.

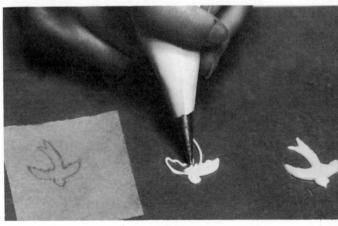

For the bluebirds, outline the shape, then fill in the outline using a fine brush to model the icing.

A small round pastry cutter provides an excellent guide for the scalloped dotted design on the top and sides of the cake. Simply rest it lightly on the cake, then make small dots in pink royal icing through a number 0 tube, spacing

81

them evenly round the cutter but not allowing them to touch it.

Place each cake on its covered board. The board for the bottom tier has a 3-inch wide ruffle of pastel pink bridal tulle attached to it.

Using a medium-sized star tube make a shell edge at the base of each cake. Carefully lift the tulle leaves and tuck them under the petals of the flowers, using dots of royal icing to keep them in place. Arrange the bluebirds in position, securing them with royal icing too.

Put the pillars on the marks you have already made on the middle and bottom tiers, and run a wooden skewer through the centre of each. It should touch the cake board. Mark the top of the skewer level with the top of the pillar, take the skewer out and cut it on the marking.

Replace it down the centre of the pillar. The skewers actually take the weight of the cake and prevent the pillars sinking into the cake.

A posy of fresh pink hyacinths and satin ribbon completes the decoration.

An ordinary pastry cutter serves as a guide for the dotted scallop trimming on the top and sides of the cake.

Three-tier Flower-decorated Wedding Cake in Clipper Work

For those who have not yet mastered pipework but want to decorate a wedding cake, clipper work is the answer. Done round the sides of a cake, and combined with moulded flowers and a minimum of pipework, it is both decorative and easy. Directions are given on page 23.

For the three tiers of the cake shown here a wedding cake mixture of 1¾ lb. butter weight (see page 135) was used. The bottom or larger tier is 10 inches in diameter, the middle tier 8 inches, and the top tier 6 inches.

The eight pillars in this cake are a little different from the usual, being made of glass. To make sure the upper tiers are firmly held, wooden skewers are run through the pillars, but to conceal them use gold or silver paper to cover the top portion of the skewer (the part that extends above the surface of the cake and is visible through the glass).

For the decoration you will need:
4 lb. almond paste
Egg white and apricot jam for glazing
5 lb. fondant icing
One quantity of royal icing
Moulded roses, hyacinths and frangipani
Bridal tulle for the covered board
8 glass pillars

Prepare the surface of each cake, trimming if necessary and brushing away any crumbs. Glaze the cake with egg white or thinned and sieved apricot jam and cover with the almond paste. Allow to stand for several days, then brush with egg white and cover with the rolled fondant.

As soon as each cake has been covered with the fondant icing, before it starts to become firm, use the clippers to make the pattern round the sides.

Mark the position of the three sprays of flowers and leave until the fondant is firm before adding the flowers and trimming with the small string scallop.

Place the cake on the prepared board, shell edge the base, and set single roses, each with a bud and leaves, at intervals on the border icing.

Place the pillars in position, run a gold- or silver-covered skewer down the centre of each, and the cake is ready to be placed on the bridal table.

A spray of frangipani and small clusters of hyacinths complete the decorations on the top tier of the cake.

Clipper work forms an easy but decorative design on this wedding cake.

Shown in colour on page 119

Five-piece Wedding Cake

As a departure from the usual tiered wedding cake try this five-piece cake. Instead of cooking the fruit cake as round or square shapes of graduated sizes, bake this one in four heart-shaped tins for the base cake, and a 6-inch round tin for the top. The top cake stands on pillars in the centre of the four heart-shaped cakes. You will need:

> A wedding cake, $1\frac{1}{2}$ lb. butter weight, baked
>   as above in five tins (see page 135)
> 4 lb. almond paste
> Egg white and apricot jam for glazing
> 6 lb. fondant icing
> One quantity of royal icing
> Piped sugar flowers
> Ribbon and tulle
> Food colourings
> 4 cake pillars

Bake the cakes at 300°F. for about 2 or $2\frac{1}{2}$ hours. If all the cakes cannot be fitted into the oven at the same time, keep the uncooked mixture in a cool place until the oven is free. It will not spoil by being allowed to stand.

Prepare the surface of the cakes by brushing away any loose crumbs after the tops have been levelled, then glaze lightly with unbeaten egg white or thinned and sieved apricot jam. Cover each cake with almond paste and allow it to stand for several days before covering with the fondant.

Divide the 6 lb. fondant icing into five equal portions. Roll each piece into a round, reserving enough to make a frill of fondant for each cake.

Brush the almond paste with unbeaten egg white and cover with the fondant (it need not come to the base of the cake). Leave this to set while you make the fondant frills.

The Fondant Frills

Take pieces of the fondant and form each into a roll: it is easier to handle a small section at a time, so have about four pieces for each cake.

Roll each piece thinly, keeping the strips as near 2 inches wide as possible. Now make a straight edge both top and bottom by cutting off the surplus icing. Use a ruler as a guide. All strips must be the same width.

Taking one piece at a time, run a thin pencil

83

*Five small cakes make this unusual wedding cake:
four are baked in heart-shaped tins, the fifth in
a 6-inch round tin. Pillars are placed on the
board, not on the cakes.*
Shown in colour on page 117

under the rolled fondant at regular intervals and,
at the same time, gently ease it to form the frill.
Press down the top edge to keep the shape. Brush
the cake lightly with unbeaten egg white and,
with the aid of a spatula, lift the frill into position
on the cake. A straight edge on the bottom of the
frill is most important.

Allow the fondant frill to become firm before
decorating the cake.

Decorating the Cake

Using a scallop pattern drawn on thin paper,
prick out scallops on the top of the cake. Pipe
their outline with royal icing through a fine
writing tube. Make the bows with the same tube.

With royal icing attach small piped flowers to
the cake where the frill of icing joins it. The

*To make the frills, roll some of the fondant and cut
into 2-inch-wide strips. Flute by running a pencil
underneath at regular intervals and pressing
down the top edge. Lift onto the cake with a
spatula.*

flowers will completely surround the round tier
but will only cover the points of the heart-shaped
cakes.

Filigree Cake Tops

Scallop and bows, made with a fine writing tube. Each scallop is about one inch wide and has a drop of no more than half an inch.

Use a satin ribbon to cover the join on the heart-shaped cakes. A dab of unbeaten egg white will keep the ribbon in place, but be sparing with it or it will stain the ribbon.

Have a large board covered with gold or silver paper. Arrange the four heart-shaped cakes with the corners of the cakes matching those of the board. When in position, stand the four cake pillars in the centre and mount the top tier.

The fresh flower posy on top is a matter of personal taste: choose any small pink or pastel-coloured flowers in season.

Place the four heart-shaped cakes in position on a large board covered with silver or gold paper. Stand the four pillars in the centre of the board to hold the round cake.

In place of the usual bouquet of flowers you may like this filigree topknot for a wedding cake.

Instead of the usual bouquet of flowers for the top of a wedding cake, an attractive decorative idea is filigree work flooded on both sides. This may be in the shape of a fan, or you may choose a simple formal design. The decoration 85 comprises four identical flooded shapes assembled on top of the cake. The picture guide shows the making of the pieces. Remember that when you choose a design for such a top decoration, the parts must not be too fragile: there should be a good percentage of heavier flooded areas, otherwise the weight of the icing will not be distributed evenly and the finer parts may crack.

Step 1: Draw the design in heavy pencil on cardboard, cover with waxed paper, and outline with royal icing through a number 0 writing tube.

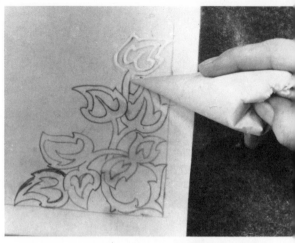

Step 2: Fill in the outline with thinned royal icing through a paper cone or a thick writing tube. A double flooding is more effective.

Attaching the Filigree Pieces to the Cake

Measure, then mark with a pin, the position of all four pieces. Make dots of royal icing through a number 1 writing tube and set the first piece in position, using the icing dots to anchor the piece.

Place a piece of cotton wool on either side of the iced shape to hold it erect. Leave until dry, then lift off the cotton wool. Mark the position of the second piece with dots of royal icing and set it in position, holding it erect with cotton wool as before.

Step 3: Remove the filigree pieces by taking the paper to the edge of the table and easing it away. Turn over each piece and flood the other side. When dry, decorate the edge of each with dots of royal icing through a number 00 writing tube.

Continue in the same way for the other two pieces, placing them one at a time in position and thus completing the filigree top.

86

Fresh Flower Posy for a Wedding Cake

A posy of fresh flowers to match those carried by the bride and her attendants makes a pretty top for a wedding cake. The picture guide and instructions show you how to make one of these posies.

Fresh flowers similar to those carried by the bride have been made into a wired posy to trim a two-tier wedding cake.
Shown in colour on page 120

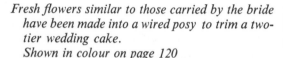

Making the wired posy. Step 1: With 26-gauge florist's wire pierce the flower through the calyx or centre.

Step 2: Bend the wire down and twist it round both itself and the stem. Cut some crepe paper into ¼-inch strips and twist them round the wire stem, stretching the paper as you wind. Make firm at the ends.

Step 3: Arrange the wired flowers into a posy, shortening the wires of some of them to produce the desired effect. Small pieces of fern or looped leaves may be wired in the same way.

Step 4: Make a ribbon bow and secure it with wire. Arrange the bow in the centre of the posy and cover the ends of the wire with ribbon or silver paper. The ends may then be pressed into the top of the cake or bent so that the posy sits flat. 87

Two-tier Christening Cake

Moulded roses and frangipani with piped forget-me-nots and a sugar stork make attractive decorations for a two-tier christening cake.

For a large christening party a double-tiered cake is the answer. Two and a half times the basic ½-lb. butter-weight mixture is needed: double the mixture is placed in a 10-inch square tin, and the remaining half basic quantity—i.e., ¼ lb. butter weight—is baked in a 4-inch by 6-inch tin. The stork on top is a sugar model which may be bought at most stores specializing in cake decorating equipment. You will need:

A rich fruit cake mixture, butter weight 1¼ lb.
   divided as above (see page 133)
3 lb. almond paste
Egg white and apricot jam for glazing
4 lb. fondant icing
One quantity of royal icing
Moulded roses and frangipani
Piped forget-me-nots
Narrow satin baby ribbon
A stork with base or stand

Make sure both cakes have a level surface. Brush them with unbeaten egg white or thinned and sieved apricot jam and cover with the almond paste, smoothing with the hands dusted with sieved icing sugar. Trim the base; leave for two or three days, then cover with the fondant icing, smoothing the surface and trimming any unevenness at the base. Allow it to become set and dry, but keep the left-over fondant in a covered container; it will be used to make the frill.

When the icing on both cakes has dried, place the small cake on top of the larger one. Roll the left-over fondant icing and make the frill for the smaller cake, as described on page 83. Attach the frill with a little unbeaten egg white.

Mould a small piece of fondant to make the pillow and place it at one end of the smaller cake.

Using a fine writing tube and royal icing in white, or coloured to match the fondant, pipe a small string scallop round the edge of the larger cake.

Change to a number 00 tube and dot the base of each fold in the fondant scallop, then make a tiny scallop pattern on the large cake where the pleated icing touches.

Lattice the fondant shape you have placed in position for the pillow, and scallop the outer edge.

Set the stork in position and trim the base with small piped or moulded roses. Add a few leaves, preferably in a light green shade.

Make a scallop design of tiny piped forget-me-nots, attaching them to the cake with dots of royal icing.

Tie a band of narrow baby ribbon so that it covers the join of the pleated icing on the small cake. Decorate the corners with small bows of the same ribbon.

Using a number 8 star tube, pipe a shell border at the base of the cake and add sprays of moulded roses, frangipani and leaves to the four corners on the board, and a single rose with leaf and tendril trim on each corner of the larger cake.

Pram Cake for a Christening

Here is a quaint idea for a christening—a cake iced as a pram and complete with sleeping "baby" and a quilted pram cover. The edible portion of the cake is the body of the pram. You will need:

> A rich fruit cake, butter weight ½ lb., baked in a 7-inch round cake tin (recipe on page 133)
> 1 lb. almond paste
> Egg white and apricot jam for glazing
> 1 lb. fondant icing
> Cardboard for the hood
> A double quantity of royal icing
> Food colourings
> Icing clippers
> 4 small wheels
> A small piece of three-ply wood or strong cardboard
> Ribbon
> Sugar flowers
> Wire for the handle

Bake the cake at 275°F. for 3½ to 4 hours. It should be made several days before it is iced and decorated.

Mark the cake across the centre, then take a line about half an inch above and cut the cake in two. You will need only the larger piece to make the pram.

Brush the cake on all sides with unbeaten egg white or thinned and sieved apricot jam, in readiness for the almond paste.

Cut the almond paste in two. Roll half into a ball, then with a rolling pin roll it into a circle. Cut in halves and use to cover the two flat sides of the cake.

Roll the remainder of the almond paste into a strip as wide as the depth of the cake, and use it to cover the rounded side and the top. Allow to stand until the following day.

Cut off about a quarter of the fondant icing. This will be used to cover the cardboard hood and to make the quilted pram cover.

Brush the almond paste with egg white and cover it with the fondant icing, using the same method of cutting and rolling as you used for the almond paste.

Let stand until the icing is set and dry.

The Pram Hood

Meanwhile, make up the cardboard shape for the hood. For this, take a rectangle of thin white

An unusual idea for a christening is a pram cake complete with pram cover and even a sleeping "baby".
Shown in colour on page 120.

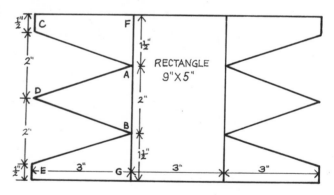

The cardboard pattern for the pram hood

cardboard 9 inches by 5 inches. With a pencil mark it crosswise into three 3-inch strips.

On strips 1 and 3 measure the extreme edges (see diagram, F and G) into 1½-inch, 2-inch and 1½-inch divisions.

On both outside edges (C and E) mark at ½-inch, 2-inch, 2-inch and ½-inch divisions. Now draw lines joining A to C and A to D, B to D, 89 and B to E. Cut along these lines and remove the triangle pieces.

Gently bend the cardboard along the line F-G. Take the points C, D and E and bring them together, overlapping them to form a point. Sew or paste these edges together.

Divide the remainder of the fondant in two. Use one half, rolled thinly, to cover the cardboard hood. Colour the other half to use for the pram quilt.

Now prepare the royal icing.

The Wickerwork

For the wickerwork on the outside of the pram you will need a number 2 writing tube.

Commencing at the top of the cake, wicker-weave the two flat sides of the cake, then pipe the rounded edge. The picture guide shows how the wickerwork pattern on the rounded ends of the pram is done. To prevent the icing breaking while the second side is being piped allow it to dry, then lay the cake on a thick pad of cotton wool.

For the semicircular sides of the pram the pattern is started with a curved line following the semicircle of the cake. Start at the rounded edge and work up to the straight edge; the semicircles will become smaller as the surface is covered. The sides and top of the pram hood are worked in the same way.

While the icing is drying, completely cover the cardboard hood with the same wickerwork icing.

The Wheels

Cover a piece of three-ply wood or strong card-board with silver paper and attach the wheels to it (you can trim the wheels with small forget-me-nots if you like).

The Pillow and Quilt

Cut off a little of the fondant icing to make a small pillow, roll the remainder to make the quilt, marking it in a diamond pattern with the back of a knife and pinching the edges with icing clippers.

Set the iced pram on the board and add the trimmings to the quilt after you have placed a small baby doll in the pram. Twist some milliner's wire for the pram handle, and tie a card with the baby's name to the handle.

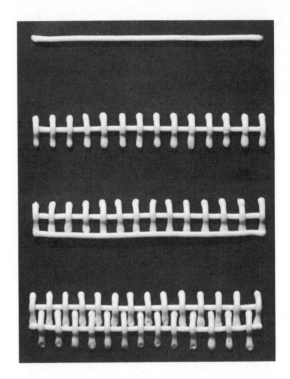

Piping the wickerwork design on the rounded ends of the pram. Step 1: With the icing bag held in a slanting position make a horizontal line along the top of the cake.
Step 2: Pipe vertical lines about half an inch in length at regular intervals over the first line.
Step 3: Pipe another horizontal line, making sure that it just covers the ends of the vertical strokes in the preceding line.
Step 4: Pipe another row of vertical lines, placing them midway between those in the row above.
Step 5: Continue in this way until the whole of the pram ends are covered.

Silver Bells and Blossoms for a 25th Wedding Anniversary

You will need:

A rich fruit cake, butter weight ½ lb., baked in an 8-inch square cake tin (recipe on page 133)
1 lb. almond paste
Egg white and apricot jam for glazing
1½ lb. fondant icing
Moulded roses and lilies
One quantity of royal icing
Food colouring
Silver colouring powder
Banana oil

Brush the cake free from crumbs and lightly glaze it with unbeaten egg white or thinned and sieved apricot jam. Cover with the rolled almond paste and leave to stand for several days.

Brush the almond covering with unbeaten egg white and cover with pale blue fondant icing. Smooth with the hands which have been dipped in sifted icing sugar, and trim the excess icing from the base with a knife. Place the cake on a covered board and leave until the icing is set and dry.

Flooded bells form the main decoration on this cake. Use the general flooding method (see page 80), double flooding the top of each bell to give it more interest. When the bells are quite dry, mix a little silver powder with some banana oil and with a fine watercolour brush run a fine line round the edge of each bell and cover the clapper. However, while the silver powder gives a decorative touch to this cake it is not edible and should be used sparingly, and then only on decorations that are easily removed before the cake is cut.

Outline the bell and bow shapes in royal icing, using a fine writing tube. Flood in the outline with royal icing thinned down with water or lemon juice.

White wedding bells edged with silver form the main decoration on this silver wedding anniversary cake.
Shown in colour on page 121

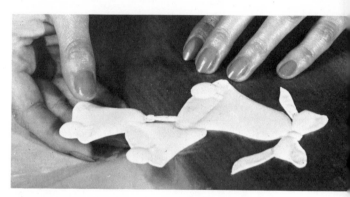

When the flooded bells are perfectly dry remove them by sliding the waxed paper to the edge of the table and carefully easing it from the bell shapes.

Arrange the flowers in an attractive spray round the bells, attaching them to the cake with dots of royal icing.

Decorate the edge with a string scallop through a fine writing tube, topping each point with a tiny leaf or a forget-me-not.

In place of the star border at the base of the cake, if you like you can use the star tube and make flat shells with the points at right angles to the board.

Using either a card or a piece of fondant icing rolled thinly and cut to a neat square, write the greeting with a fine watercolour brush in vegetable colouring.

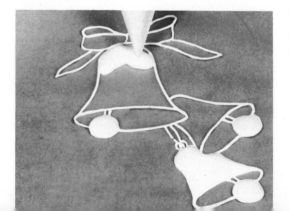

91

Rose-decorated Cake for a Silver Wedding Anniversary

You will need:

> A rich fruit cake, butter weight ½ lb., baked in an 8-inch square cake tin (recipe on page 133)
> Egg white and apricot jam for glazing
> 1 lb. almond paste
> 1½ lb. fondant icing
> Moulded roses
> Piped forget-me-nots
> Flooded bells
> Lacework
> Ribbon
> One quantity of royal icing
> Food colourings

Cover the cake with the rolled almond paste, first brushing it with unbeaten egg white or thinned and sieved apricot jam. Leave for several days, then glaze with unbeaten egg white and cover with 1¼ lb. of the fondant icing tinted a pastel blue. Leave to dry before decorating.

Colour the remaining ¼ lb. of the fondant icing a strong pink and mould it into roses. You will need about six or seven for the top decoration, four larger roses for the corners of the cake, and about 18 buds. Leave the roses to become set and dry.

On waxed paper, and using a number 00 writing tube, pipe 24 lace motifs (see page 95 for piping lace). When the lace is quite dry, attach it to the sides and top of the cake as shown in the picture.

Make the flooded bells in white icing and when dry, attach them to the cake with royal icing. Arrange the roses at the top and bottom of the bells, and add a few forget-me-nots—these may be piped directly onto the cake in pastel pink or white royal icing, or piped on waxed paper and then transferred to the cake.

Pipe a single scallop of white royal icing round the edge of the cake and write "Congratulations" with the same icing and tube.

Arrange the roses and buds on the four corners of the cake, then pipe a shell border using a number 8 star tube. Colour the remainder of the icing pale green and add small piped leaves to the roses on the top and corners of the cake.

Finish the decoration with a bow of pale blue satin ribbon.

A pale-blue satin ribbon makes a pretty contrast to the pink and green of this rose-decorated cake for a silver wedding anniversary.
Shown in colour on page 121

Outline and flood the small bells, then emboss the surface.

Apricot-tinted Cake for a Silver Wedding Anniversary

You will need:

> *A rich fruit cake, butter weight ½ lb., baked in an 8-inch round tin (recipe on page 133)*
> *1 lb. almond paste*
> *Egg white and apricot jam for glazing*
> *1½ lb. fondant icing*
> *One quantity of royal icing*
> *Moulded leaves and flowers (with flower stamens)*
> *Pink and yellow food colourings*

Brush the cake free from crumbs, glaze with un-beaten egg white or thinned and sieved apricot jam and then cover with the rolled almond paste. Allow to stand for several days.

Take about ¼ lb. of the white fondant and set it aside for moulding the roses and leaves.

Add a few drops of both yellow and pink colouring to the 1¼ lb. white fondant and knead evenly to make a pastel apricot shade.

Brush the cake with unbeaten egg white and cover with the apricot fondant icing. Trim the base with a sharp knife and leave the icing to become firm before decorating.

The Rose and Leaves

This cake is decorated with single roses moulded from the ¼ lb. white fondant icing. Work it well with the fingers until it is pliable, then break off six small pieces for the six petals of each rose. Model each into a rose petal shape.

Place pieces of waxed paper about 1½ inches in diameter in the bottom of metal patty-cake pans. On the paper in one of these little cake recesses arrange the six petals to form an open or single rose. Each one should slightly overlap the other. A tiny dab of water or unbeaten egg white applied with the tip of a fine watercolour brush may be used to stick the petals together. Make as many of these single roses as you need, then leave until set and dry.

Colour a small quantity of royal icing yellow and, using a fine writing tube, dot the centre of each rose. While this is still soft, attach small millinery stamens. Leave until dry.

Make the leaves from the same fondant, shaping them with the fingers and marking the veins with the back edge of a small knife or with

Simplicity is the keynote of this silver wedding design. The cake is iced in a delicate shade of apricot.
Shown in colour on page 122

a fine skewer. For a more interesting shape, dry the leaves over a pencil or the handle of a wooden spoon.

The Lettering

It isn't always easy for the beginner to pipe words or numerals directly onto a cake. To avoid spoiling your cake with poor lettering, trace the figures or the letters on a piece of thick paper or thin cardboard, cover this with waxed paper and follow the outlines in royal icing through a fine writing tube. Flood each outline with more icing, allow to dry, then cover with small dots of royal icing through a fine writing tube.

Let the icing become quite dry, then slide the words or figures off the waxed paper and attach to the cake with a little white royal icing.

The Finishing Decorations

Decorate the side of the cake with scallops of fine dots made with royal icing, and trim the base where the cake meets the board with a star border made with royal icing through a number 8 tube.

93

Rose Appliqué Design for a Silver Wedding Anniversary

The cake for this design is a ½ lb. butter-weight rich fruit cake baked in an 8-inch square tin and covered with almond and fondant icing—the same as in the apricot-tinted cake just described except for the shape of the cake. With a bold design in the rose appliqué, the other trimmings are restrained—simply a filigree butterfly and some sugar lace. Large dots of icing are placed close together right round the edge of the cake, which stands on a silver-covered board with a tulle frill. The accompanying picture with its caption shows you how to make the rose and leaves; you will find instructions for the sugar lacework and the butterfly on pages 95 and 96.

With the waxed paper pinned securely over the pencilled design, outline the rose and leaves with well-worked royal icing through a fine writing tube.

The bold rose appliqué design on this silver wedding anniversary cake is set off with a simple filigree butterfly and a little sugar lacework.
Shown in colour on page 122

Filigree Work and Flooding

Fine filigree or lacework will add a touch of elegance to your decorated cakes. With practice, no design is beyond the scope of even the amateur decorator, but you must have well-worked free-flowing icing and a fine writing tube.

In some cases the filigree design is piped directly onto the cake. Sometimes the design—especially when it is to be placed on the cake at an angle, or as a border—is completed on paper, then lifted off carefully and arranged on the cake.

Flooding is useful when you want to raise or emphasize the whole or part of a design. As with the filigree, it may be done either directly on the cake or on waxed paper from which it is lifted off when dry and then placed on the cake.

Only royal icing is suitable for filigree or lace-work or flooding work.

SUGAR LACE EDGING

Some of the daintiest effects, especially for wedding and christening cakes, are achieved when sugar lace edgings are incorporated in the design.

Only royal icing is suited to this type of work. A small quantity of liquid glucose, one teaspoonful to one egg white, will make the icing softer and more pliable.

Make sure you beat the royal icing by hand for this type of work. An electric beater tends to beat too much air into the icing and there is a risk of the air bubbles breaking while you are piping the fine lines.

Select any one of the patterns given on this page, trace it on a piece of paper and place it on a work board. Cover with waxed paper. If you have the pattern on a thin strip of paper you can draw it across and use the same outline for the whole edging.

Using a number 0 writing tube and well-worked royal icing trace the outline, making sure that it joins up at all points. Unless this is done the lace will break when being taken from the waxed paper.

The beginner will find the traced outline a help, but as she becomes more proficient the lace shapes can be done freehand, since it is not necessary for them to be perfectly uniform. They are very delicate and need to be handled carefully. You are sure to break a few, either removing them from the paper or attaching them to the cake, so make a few more than you need.

Removing the Lace from the Paper and Attaching it to the Cake

Be sure each little pattern is perfectly dry before attempting to remove it from the paper: leave overnight if possible.

There are two ways to remove them. Either slide a thin-bladed knife under each lace motif, or bend the paper slightly from the back and

Here are eight designs for sugar lacework, shown actual size. Choose one and trace it on paper, using a heavy pencil.

ease the shapes off with the fingernail.

To attach the lace to the cake use a line of small dots of the same royal icing through a fine writing tube.

These lace motifs can stand upright or be arranged at an angle, depending on the cake design.

FLOODED APPLIQUÉ WORK

With this type of decorative icing you have the opportunity of adding a truly personal touch to your cakes, especially wedding or anniversary cakes.

You can reproduce the lace motifs from a bride's dress by tracing them on waxed paper and using them as part of the decoration on her wedding cake. This idea offers wonderful scope for the clever decorator.

Reproducing a Lace Design in Icing

Place a piece of the lace with the main motif on a firm surface. Cover it with tracing paper. Outline the design in pencil on the tracing paper. Now remove the lace and, with a heavier pencil, make a clear outline of the lace pattern.

Place this tracing on a work board, cover with a piece of waxed paper, then secure both to the board with drawing pins.

Have ready some well-worked royal icing and a number 00 writing tube. Following the pencilled outline, reproduce the design in fine piping on the waxed paper.

A fine pointed watercolour brush will help correct any irregularities in the icing and will enable you to join the ends neatly.

Now thin down the royal icing with a little

Thin down some royal icing with lemon juice or water, and flood in the outline. Use a fine water-colour brush to ease the icing into the corners.

water or lemon juice to a stage where it will run freely, or "flood".

Place this soft icing in a bag with a number 2 writing tube attached, then flood in the pattern with it. Here again you can call on your fine watercolour brush to help you ease it evenly into the corners, curves and narrow sections of the pattern.

For a better effect some parts of the design can be made higher than others: this is achieved by a second flooding, but be sure the first flooding is quite dry before adding the second layer.

Veins in the leaves can be made by drawing the point of the brush through the icing as it is setting.

Should you wish to add dots or edgings to the appliqué, wait until the entire surface is perfectly dry, then use a royal icing of the usual writing consistency.

Removing the Appliqué from the Paper

This must be done very carefully. Place the paper on which you have flooded the design near the edge of the table. Gently pull the paper in a downward direction. It will come away from the icing, leaving the design intact.

A few dots on the back of the motif will keep it in position on the cake.

LINE OR FLOODED BUTTERFLIES

Butterflies may be made either with an unfilled outline, i.e. in filigree, or a flooded outline: it depends on the design you have chosen for the cake.

Use a free-flowing royal icing and trace the design on waxed paper.

If only the outline is required, as in the colour picture on page 122, simply leave to dry, then carefully lift off and attach to the cake with tiny dots of royal icing.

For the flooded type, fill in the outline with softened royal icing and leave to become dry and set. Attach to the cake with royal icing.

Making line or flooded butterflies

Pale Pink Lacy Cake for a Silver Wedding Anniversary

You will need:

> A rich fruit cake, butter weight ½ lb., baked in an 8-inch round cake tin (recipe on page 133)
> 1 lb. almond paste
> Egg white and apricot jam for glazing
> 1½ lb. pale pink fondant icing
> Tulle
> Piped roses, jonquils and forget-me-nots
> One quantity of royal icing
> Food colourings

Brush the cake with unbeaten egg white or thinned and sieved apricot jam and cover with the almond paste. Leave for two or three days, then brush with egg white and cover with the fondant icing rolled to an even thickness. Smooth with the hands which have been dusted with sifted icing sugar, trim the base and leave for a day for the icing to dry.

Meanwhile make the piped flowers, the tulle ruffle and the flooded number 25.

The tulle ruffle. Cut a piece of pink tulle about 2½ inches wide and 8 inches long. Run a drawing thread along one side. Draw or trace a simple lace design on a piece of waxed paper, place it on a board, cover with the tulle strip and pin securely with paper pins. Using a soft royal icing through a fine writing tube, outline the lace pattern on the tulle. While the icing is still soft gather the drawing thread to make the ruffle. Secure the ends of the thread, cut off neatly and arrange the ruffle in the centre of the cake. Do not work on the rest of the decoration until the tulle icing is quite dry.

Decorating the Cake

Divide the top of the cake into five equal sections. Arrange a spray of roses, jonquils, forget-me-nots and roses at each point and trim with small green leaves through your smallest leaf tube.

Use a number 00 tube and pink royal icing to scallop the edge of the cake, making the scallop under the flower spray a little deeper than those between the flowers.

Change to a star tube and shell edge the base of the cake, adding a rose and leaves at intervals on the shell.

For more interest, the flooded number 25 in

A simple lace design piped on pink tulle is one of the prettiest features of this silver wedding cake. Shown in colour on page 123

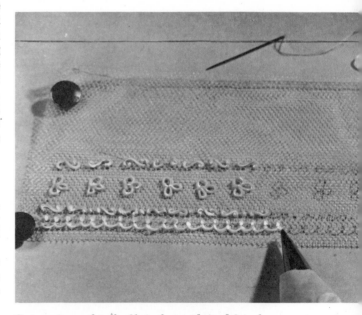

Cut a piece of tulle 2½ inches wide and 8 inches long, run a drawing thread along one edge, pipe the lace design with a fine writing tube, and gather up the ruffle while the icing is still soft. 97

this design has been covered with tiny forget-me-nots, added after the figures have dried.

Stand the number in the centre of the tulle ruffle, keeping the figures in place with royal icing and supporting them with small pads of cotton wool until the icing has dried.

These numbers are very fragile and must be handled carefully. To remove them from the paper, place it on the edge of the table and gently ease it from the back of the dried figures. A little fresh icing holds the figures in position on the cake.

Trace the numbers 2 and 5 in heavy pencil on a piece of strong paper, cover with waxed paper and pin to the board. Outline the figures in royal icing through a fine writing tube and allow to become partly dry.

Golden Wedding Cake

The size of the cake will vary according to the number of people invited to celebrate the golden wedding—in this case it was a rich wedding cake mixture with a butter weight of 1¼ lb. and the other ingredients in proportion, and was baked in an 11-inch round cake tin (see page 135).

As well as the cake you will need:

> 2 lb. almond paste
> 3 lb. cream-coloured fondant icing (this is sufficient to make roses and leaves as well as covering the cake)
> Egg white and apricot jam for glazing
> 7 large moulded roses for the top of the cake, 7 smaller ones for the cameos
> 7 flooded oval shapes
> Lace edgings piped in white royal icing
> One quantity of royal icing
> Tulle ruffle for the cake board

With water or lemon juice thin down some of the royal icing. With a thicker writing tube or a paper icing bag without a tube fill in the outline, easing the icing into the corners with a brush. Allow to dry overnight.

Cover the cake with almond paste, first glazing it with thinned and sieved apricot jam. Let it stand for one week. Take 2½ lb. of the fondant icing and knead, then roll out. Brush the cake with unbeaten egg white and cover with the fondant, removing any excess icing from the base. Let it become quite dry before decorating.

The Cameos

The cameos are made separately and attached to the cake when they are dry. Take a piece of paper and draw an oval shape 2 inches in length and $1\frac{1}{4}$ inches wide. Outline with royal icing through a fine writing tube.

Thin down some royal icing and with the aid of a fine watercolour brush fill in the oval outline. Leave until set and dry. Seven cameos are required for this size cake. The lace edgings for the cameos are made in the usual way, but to make sure they will fit snugly round the oval shape, trace an oval the same size as those that have been flooded and using it as a pattern outline pipe the fine lace edge round it. Make a few more than seven of these edgings because you are sure to break some.

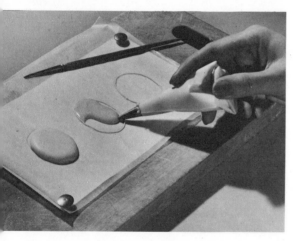

The cameos for the side decorations are made separately. Outline ovals 2 inches long and $1\frac{1}{4}$ inches wide at the centre, flood in, and allow to dry.

To make sure the lace edging will fit snugly round the cameos, trace an oval the same size as the one that has been flooded, and pipe the lace round it.

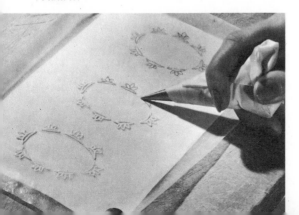

Rose cameos trimmed with lace and ruffled ribbon bows make eyecatching decorations on this golden wedding cake.
Shown in colour on page 123

The Larger Roses and the Leaves

It is a little more difficult to mould the larger roses than the smaller ones. To keep the petals a good shape allow them to become partly dry before putting them together. But you must be careful not to let them dry too much, or they will crack when being handled. Use the same fondant as that used for covering the cake, but work it well with your fingers to make it more pliable. Take small pieces and mould them into petals, using your thumb to hollow them out slightly. (As a guide for the shape of the petals, pull a real rose to pieces.) At least ten petals are required for each rose, plus a centre which is made by rolling a piece of the fondant into a cylindrical shape. Around this shape arrange the pear-shaped petals, lightly brushing the ends with unbeaten egg white to make them stick. To keep the roses a good shape dry them in small patty tins lined on the bottom with small pieces of waxed paper.

Shape the leaves from the same coloured fondant and leave them to dry over the handle of a wooden spoon. This gives a curled, more interesting shape to the leaves.

99

Moulded roses for the centre of each cake are set to dry in patty tins to keep them a good shape. The leaves are curved by drying them over the handle of a wooden spoon.

Decorating the Cake

Measure the cake, mark it into 7 equal parts and place a flooded oval cameo in each, attaching it to the cake with a little royal icing.

Add the lacework to the outside edge of each cameo and place a small moulded rose in the centre of each. Green leaves moulded from the same fondant will improve the appearance of the rosebuds.

On the rounded edge of the cake, and between the cameos, pipe bows, using a thin ribbon tube.

Set the moulded roses in the centre of the cake and arrange the leaves around them.

Mount the cake on a board covered with gold paper and edged with a tulle ruffle and decorate the base of the cake with overlapping moulded roses.

The number 50 is flooded on waxed paper and when dry attached to the cake.

100

Happy Christmas Cake

Holly leaves and candles for a gay Christmas cake

You will need a $\frac{1}{2}$-lb. butter-weight rich fruit cake (recipe on page 133), baked in an 8-inch round cake tin.

Brush the cake with egg white or thinned and sieved apricot jam and cover with the almond paste in the usual way. Allow to stand for two or three days, then brush with unbeaten egg white and cover with the rolled fondant. Smooth the surface and trim any excess icing from the base of the cake. Allow to become set before decorating.

Measure round the outside of the cake, mark at one-inch intervals and, using a well-worked royal icing, make a string scallop round the cake.

Fill in the area between the scallops and the base of the cake with small dots of royal icing through a number 1 writing tube.

Add a shell border with the same icing, using a number 8 star tube.

Now mark the top of the cake into four equal divisions. In royal icing outline then flood a candle, with its flame towards the centre of the cake. Outline three holly leaves at the base of each candle.

Join up the four candles with half scallops of royal icing, then colour the remainder of the icing red.

Make three dots through a number 2 writing tube for the holly, then outline and flood the "Happy Christmas" greeting in the centre.

Using a fine watercolour brush, paint the flame of the candle in yellow and red colourings.

Marzipan Christmas Cake

Marzipan fruits and clipper work are all you need in the way of decoration on this simple Christmas cake.

Shown in colour on page 124

One round of fondant on top of the cake, decorated with clipper work, is the basis of this simple Christmas design. Make a rich fruit cake of butter weight ½ lb., baked in an 8-inch round tin (recipe on page 133).

The fruits are made of marzipan or almond paste. Mould the paste according to the shapes desired, then allow to dry. With a fine watercolour brush and food colourings, tint the fruits in their natural colours.

At the blossom end of each apple or pear put a little piece of clove, and at the other end a longer piece to represent the stem, also one on the apricots.

Mark the moulded pineapple and bananas by streaking with brown colouring. Make the leaves from the uncoloured almond paste, then, when dry, paint the undiluted colour on them. Leave until dry before placing on the cake. A little egg white or a dab of royal icing will keep them in place.

Christmas Tree Cake

Christmas bells and flooded Christmas trees make an effective decoration for this cake. It is suitable for either a ½-lb. or a 1-lb. butter-weight rich fruit mixture (basic recipe on page 133), baked in an 8-inch or 10-inch round cake tin. If used for a pound mixture baked in a 10-inch cake tin, allow 1½ lb. almond paste and 2 lb. fondant. If used for a ½ lb. mixture baked in an 8-inch tin allow 1 lb. almond and 1½ lb. fondant. As well as the almond paste and fondant icing you will need royal icing, ribbon bows and food colourings.

Cover the cake with the almond paste in the usual way, then with the fondant icing. Divide the royal icing in two. Leave one half white. Divide the remainder in two and colour one part green and the other red.

Make four sets of flooded bells (see pages 79, 80). Leave these to dry.

Trace the outline of two small fir trees directly on the cake or on waxed paper, then with a pin or a fine skewer prick the outline onto the cake. Colour one of the smaller portions of icing green and use it to outline then flood the trees, using number 1 writing tube.

With white royal icing pipe a shell border at the base of the cake, using a number 8 star tube.

Measure round the edge of the cake and mark at one-inch intervals, then string scallop a border with a number 00 writing tube, using the marks as a guide.

While you have the white royal icing in the tube, dot the top of the cake as shown in the photograph, then make two wavy lines under the trees.

101

With the red royal icing and the number 1 tube over-scallop a border on the white border you already have on the edge of the cake.

Attach the bells to the four corners of the cake, and when dry trim with small ribbon bows.

A cake for Christmas featuring Christmas bells and fir trees

Christmas Greeting Cake

This design is suitable for either a 1-lb. butter-weight cake baked in a 10-inch round cake tin, or a ½-lb. butter-weight cake baked in an 8-inch round cake tin (recipe on page 133). The quantities given here are for the larger cake. You will need:

> 1½ lb. almond paste
> Egg white or apricot jam for glazing
> 2 lb. fondant icing
> One quantity of royal icing

> Moulded roses
> Food colourings

Cover the cake with the almond paste after brushing with unbeaten egg white or thinned and sieved apricot jam. Leave for two or three days, then cover with the fondant icing.

Re-roll the scraps of fondant icing and put a little aside to make the roses. Divide the remainder in two. Roll each piece between the hands to the thickness of a cord (about ¼ inch) and twist it together. Use this as the decoration on the base of the cake, applying it as soon as the covering icing has been applied.

Colour the fondant with food colouring and mould into roses.

Measure round the cake and mark it in equal parts. Using a fine star tube, make a shell scallop round the top edge of the cake.

Place the roses in a semi-circle about a quarter of the way in from the edge of the cake. Decorate with two-tone leaves and a few tendrils and dots.

Write the Christmas greeting in brown coloured royal icing.

A semicircle of moulded roses and two-tone leaves makes an attractive decoration for a Christmas cake.

Shown in colour on page 124

Flower decorations piped through a petal tube with royal icing   page 16

Log Cabin Cake   page 27

Clown Cake   page 28

Dolly Varden Cake   page 29

Easter Bunny Cake page 30

Duck Cake page 33

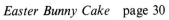

Gipsy Caravan Cake page 32

105

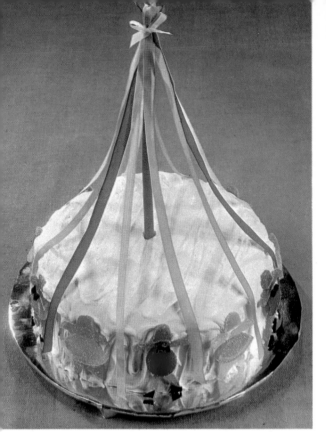

Maypole Cake page 34

Guardsman Cake page 35

Drum Cake page 38

106

Chocolate Box Cake   page 39

Wagon Train   page 42

Hat-box Cake   page 43

Gingerbread Children   page 44

Birthday Express   page 46

108

For a children's party: sailing ships, little duck-lings and small iced cakes   page 47

Storybook cookies are fun for all the family to make   page 50

Telegram Cake for Dad   page 51

Grape and Lattice Cake   page 52

Say it with Flowers   page 53

110

Yellow Rose Cake   page 53

Wisteria Cake   page 55

Posy Cake for Grandma   page 55

111

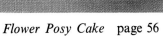

Flower Posy Cake   page 56

Basket of Roses   page 57

Daisy Cake   page 58

Teenager's Dream Cake   page 59

Spring flowers for a 21st birthday   page 60

113

Two-tier 21st birthday cake   page 62
Key-shaped 21st birthday cake for a boy   page 62

Silver keys and shaded roses for a 21st birthday
page 66

Miniature fruits on a 21st birthday cake   page 66

Key-shaped 21st birthday cake for a girl   page 62

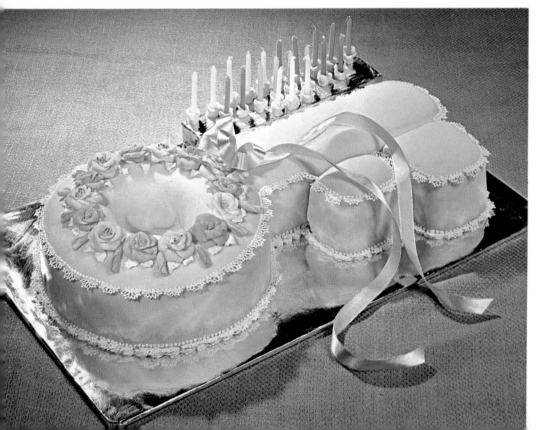

115

Engagement cake   page 67

Two-tier Pink Rose wedding cake   page 71

Simple elegance for a wedding cake page 69

Five-piece wedding cake page 83

117

Three-tier heart-shaped wedding cake   page 80

Three-tier flower-decorated wedding cake in clipper work   page 82

119

Fresh flower posy for a wedding cake   page 87

Pram Cake for a christening   page 89

Silver bells and blossoms for a 25th wedding anniversary   page 91

Rose-decorated cake for a silver wedding anniversary   page 92

Apricot-tinted cake for a silver wedding anniversary page 93

Rose appliqué design for a silver wedding anniversary page 94

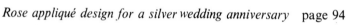

Pale pink lacy cake for a silver wedding anniversary page 97

Golden wedding cake page 98

123

Marzipan Christmas Cake page 101

Christmas Greeting Cake page 102

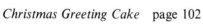

124

Christmas Bell Cake page 127

Tea-tree Flowers Christmas Cake page 128

Pink Vienna icing (page 131) covers the top and sides of this sponge sandwich. The same icing is used for the piped decorations, and fresh fruit makes a trimming.

Little party cakes   page 131

Christmas Bell Cake

Red candles, pink and white bells, and holly decorate this colourful Christmas cake. Shown in colour on page 125

You will need:

> *A rich fruit cake, butter weight ½ lb., baked in an 8-inch round cake tin (recipe on page 133)*
> *1 lb. almond paste*
> *Egg white and apricot jam for glazing*
> *1½ lb. white fondant icing*
> *One quantity of royal icing*
> *Pink sugar bells and white flooded bells*
> *Food colourings*

If necessary, trim the top of the cake to make it level, brush away any crumbs, and glaze lightly with egg white or thinned and sieved apricot jam. Cover with the almond paste rolled to an even thickness.

Leave for two or three days before covering with the fondant icing.

A light brushing of egg white will make the fondant icing cling to the almond covering. Roll the white fondant, then cover the cake with it, smoothing with the hands dusted with sifted icing sugar. Leave until set before decorating.

The day before decorating the cake, make the flooded bells (see pages 79, 80) and the pink sugar bells (instructions follow).

The Sugar Bells

To 1½ cups of sugar add half an unbeaten egg white and about 10 drops of red food colouring. Blend the colouring into the sugar with the back of a spoon, then squeeze the mixture in your hand. If it leaves the imprint of your fingers it is moist enough. If too dry, add a few drops of water.

Pack the sugar into bell-shaped moulds (see picture) and stand each filled mould on waxed paper. Tap the bell gently then lift off the mould. If the mixture sticks, it is too wet, so add more sugar and repack the mould. It won't hold its shape if it is too dry. After turning the bell out of the mould allow to harden for about one hour.

Making sugar bells. Step 1: Pack the prepared coloured sugar mixture into bell-shaped moulds.

Step 2: Stand the filled mould on waxed paper and tap the bell gently.

127

Now carefully scrape the moist sugar from the inside of the bell, leaving a wall about one-eighth of an inch in thickness. Should the first bell you attempt to scrape out crumble, leave the others to dry a little longer.

Poke a small hole in the top of each bell, then, if you wish, string a small Christmas ball through the hole for the bell clapper.

Step 3: Leave to harden, then scrape out the centre of each with a pointed knife.

Decorating the Cake

Measure round the sides of the cake and mark evenly into eight sections. Arrange a pair of flooded bells at each mark. Run two shallow scallops in white royal icing between each pair of bells, using a fine writing tube.

Pipe a shell border in white royal icing at the base of the cake.

Colour the remainder of the royal icing a bright red for flooding the candles.

Mark the position of the sugar bells and the candle on the top of the cake, but do not place the bells in position at this stage.

Using a fine skewer, outline the shape of three candles with the red royal icing through a fine writing tube: the taller candle should be in the centre. Thin down the icing and flood in each candle. Leave a tiny space at the top of each, and with a fine watercolour brush paint a flame for each candle in yellow, then a wick in black.

Place the bells in position on the cake, add clappers of black icing if liked, and pipe the greetings in black royal icing through a number 00 tube.

For the holly leaves on the sides and top of the cake, use scraps of white fondant, rolling and cutting it for the leaves and making small balls for the holly berries.

Brush the undiluted colouring on these, using a fine pointed watercolour brush.

Tea-tree Flowers Christmas Cake

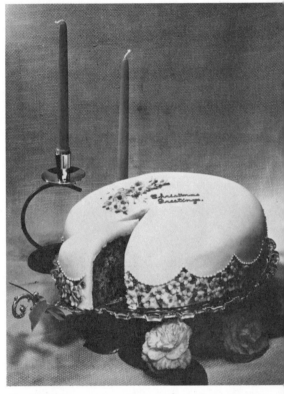

A Christmas cake design featuring tea-tree blossoms
Shown in colour on page 125

Bright pink Australian tea-tree blossoms have been used for the decoration on this Christmas cake. You may have either a full 1-lb. butter-weight fruit cake or a ½-lb. butter-weight one (recipe on page 133).

To cover the cake follow the instructions given for the Christmas Greeting Cake.

In place of roses you'll need dozens of tea-tree flowers. These are moulded in pale pink, and

128

centres are painted a deeper colour with a fine watercolour brush.

Instead of having piped scallops round the outside of the cake, form scallops with dots of royal icing piped with a number 1 writing tube.

Fill in the area between the scallops and the base of the cake with flowers, and pipe small leaves between the blossoms.

Moulded tea-tree blossoms make a spray on top of the cake, and the Christmas greeting is piped in brown royal icing through a number 0 writing tube.

Edible crystallized violets, cinerarias, and hyacinths top off squares of plain cake covered with butter cream icing.

Crystallized Flowers

Fresh flowers have always been popular for a decorative touch on a cake, but they wilt quickly and may only be used for a short period. A simple way to preserve blossoms and at the same time make them edible is to crystallize them. Small flowers, especially those that bloom in the spring, may be sugared and stored in air-tight containers for several months. They will not lose their colours.

Violets, polyanthus, hyacinths, single stock and small cinerarias are suitable, or other small flowers with solid centres. Rose petals crystallize well, too.

Take one egg white and mix it with one tablespoon of water. Have ready a piece of greaseproof paper sprinkled with caster sugar. Pick the flowers (they must be absolutely fresh) then with a watercolour brush lightly coat their surfaces with the egg white and water mixture. Don't put on too thick a coat, but make sure every part has been covered. Now lay each flower in the sugar on the paper and sprinkle more sugar over until the flower is lightly and evenly coated.

Place the sugared flowers on a tray and leave in an airy place to dry. Avoid a damp atmosphere and let the flowers dry naturally. They will be ready to store after a couple of days, or when they are crisp and thoroughly dry.

Use for small cakes and for confectionery.

Chocolate Leaves

Whether you use them on a sponge cake, on ice cream, or on a very special dessert, chocolate leaves provide an edible and interesting decoration.

Dark eating or cooking chocolate should be used. Be careful not to overheat it, or it will become discoloured. Milk chocolate is not suitable.

Choose rose leaves or small lemon leaves with well-defined veins, for they show up the best when the chocolate has set and is peeled off. When picking them, be sure to leave a little of the stem—it will make the handling much easier.

Rinse the leaves and dry them well before commencing to work with the chocolate.

Heat some dark eating or cooking chocolate over hot (not boiling) water. When it begins to melt, remove from the heat and beat until smooth.

Using a new watercolour brush, thickly paint the undersides of the leaves with a smooth but thick coating of chocolate, spreading it just to the edges. Refrigerate the leaves until the chocolate is firm.

129

Removing the leaves. Insert the tip of a pointed knife at the tip of the leaf. As you peel the real leaf off, quickly place the chocolate leaf on waxed paper. You must be quick but gentle when handling them, for the chocolate melts rapidly with the heat of the fingers.

Keep refrigerated until required.

Step 2: When the chocolate has dried, insert the tip of a pointed knife at the tip of the leaf, and peel off the real leaf from the chocolate shape.

Cover the top of the sponge with a butter icing, then trim with chilled chocolate leaves and pieces of orange.

Making chocolate leaves. Step 1: Using a water-colour brush, thickly paint the undersides of rose leaves with melted chocolate.

Warm or Glacé Icing

    4 oz. sifted icing sugar
    1 tablespoon water, milk or fruit juice
    Food colouring

Place the sifted icing sugar in an enamel saucepan. Add the liquid, stirring until smooth. Place the saucepan over medium heat for about 10 seconds, stirring well with a wooden spoon. Colour as required.

If water or milk are used, the icing may be flavoured with vanilla essence if you like.

Pour quickly over the cake, smoothing with a broad-bladed knife which has been dipped in hot water.

This is sufficient to cover the top of a cake baked in a 7-inch cake tin or an orange loaf tin.

Chocolate Glacé Icing

Sift 2 level tablespoons of cocoa with 4 oz. icing sugar, mix with 1 tablespoon water and flavour with vanilla. With the extra cocoa you may need an extra teaspoon of water. To make the icing glossy, add one teaspoon of melted butter or half a teaspoon of glycerine. Be careful not to overheat chocolate icing or it will be a light colour when it dries.

Vienna Icing

3 oz. soft butter
8 oz. sifted icing sugar
About 3 tablespoons orange juice or milk
Cream the butter until smooth, then gradually beat in the icing sugar and the milk or fruit juice. Colour as preferred.

Chocolate Vienna Icing

Add 2 rounded tablespoons cocoa to the icing sugar before sifting, and use sherry or rum in place of the milk or fruit juice.

Little Party Cakes

A rich butter cake or plain cake (recipe on page 48) is best for these little decorated party cakes. Make the cake mixture the day before the cakes are to be iced and decorated, for they will be easier to handle. Glacé icing is used to cover them, and small piped roses or other flowers, or moulded marzipan fruits, together with piped royal icing, is used for decorating.

For raised cream work on little cakes, make up some butter icing (see page 36) and pipe the butter cream shapes directly onto the cakes. Place them in the refrigerator and chill until the butter cream is very firm, then coat with the glacé icing.

In some cases it is possible to make these chilled cream cakes into fruit shapes. While the glacé icing is still soft, add a dab of pure food colouring, then streak it lightly with the tip of a watercolour brush to represent a pear or an apple. Break a clove in half, use the blossom end for the blossom end of the fruit, and the little piece of stalk for the fruit stem. Pipe a few leaves in green or two-toned brown and green royal icing at the stem end, or round the fruit shape.

For the glacé icing, sift 1¼ lb. of icing sugar into a saucepan and stir in 6 tablespoons of water or fruit juice.

Divide the icing according to the number of colours you will require to ice these little cakes. Tint one quantity at a time, heat it and pour quickly over the cakes. Allow this icing to set,

then decorate with flowers, fruit and royal icing.

If you want a chocolate coating for some of the cakes ice them last so that you can gather up all the icing you have left, mix the colours in the one saucepan and add a tablespoon of cocoa. You may need a little more liquid. Heat this chocolate icing briefly, then use to coat the little cakes.

A delightful assortment of little party cakes
Shown in colour on page 126

Petit-fours

These are made with the same butter cake mixture and the same glacé icing, but it is usual to make them very much smaller and to coat each little cake with a very thin layer of almond paste before adding the glacé icing. The flowers should be miniature ones, and the pipework done with the smallest of icing tubes.

131

Sponge Sandwich

4 eggs
A pinch of salt
4 oz. sugar
½ teaspoon vanilla essence
4 oz. plain flour
1 level teaspoon cream of tartar
1 teaspoon butter
1 tablespoon hot water
½ level teaspoon bicarbonate of soda

Prepare two 7-inch sandwich tins by greasing well and then lining the bottom of each with a round of greased paper.

Separate the egg whites from the yolks. Add the salt to the whites and beat until soft peaks form. Gradually add the sugar and continue beating until thick and glossy. Add the egg yolks one at a time, and flavour with vanilla.

Sift the flour with the cream of tartar three times. Melt the butter in the hot water and add the soda. Stir until it has dissolved.

Fold the sifted flour into the egg mixture, using a wooden spoon, and then lightly stir in the melted butter and water and the soda.

Place the cake mixture in the prepared tins and bake in a moderate oven, temperature 350° F., for 20 to 25 minutes.

Turn out onto a cake cooler and remove the paper.

Light Fruit Cake

1 cup sultanas
1 cup seeded raisins
¼ cup chopped cherries
¼ cup chopped mixed peel
¼ cup chopped blanched almonds
½ lb. butter
½ lb. sugar
4 eggs
12 oz. plain flour
3 level teaspoons baking powder
A pinch of salt
1 level teaspoon nutmeg
1 level teaspoon mixed spice
2 tablespoons milk
2 tablespoons brandy

Prepare the fruit and nuts. Line an 8-inch cake tin with two thicknesses of brown and two of white paper.

Cream together the butter and sugar until light and fluffy. Add the eggs one at a time, beating well after each addition. Stir in the fruit and nuts. Sift the flour with the baking powder, salt and spices and stir into the mixture alternately with the milk and brandy.

Place in the prepared tin and bake in a moderate oven, 325°F., for about 2¼ hours.

Marble Cake

6 oz. butter
6 oz. white sugar
½ teaspoon vanilla essence
3 eggs
12 oz. self-raising flour
¼ teaspoon salt
¾ cup milk
Cochineal
1 tablespoon cocoa

Beat the butter and sugar to a cream and flavour with the vanilla. Beat the eggs until twice their original size and add gradually to the mixture, beating well after each addition.

Sift the flour with the salt and add to the creamed mixture alternately with the milk.

Divide the mixture into three equal portions. Leave one plain, colour the second with a few drops of cochineal, and add the cocoa to the third.

Place in alternate spoonfuls in a well-greased 8-inch round cake tin and bake in a moderate oven, 350°F., for about 50 minutes.

Rich Fruit Cake

Basic ½-lb. Butter-weight Recipe

½ lb. butter
¼ lb. light brown sugar
¼ lb. white sugar
4 eggs
4 tablespoons brandy, whisky or sherry
10 oz. plain flour
½ level teaspoon mixed spice
½ level teaspoon baking powder
½ level teaspoon nutmeg
A good pinch of salt
½ lb. sultanas
¼ lb. mixed peel
2 oz. cherries
½ lb. seeded raisins
¼ lb. currants
¼ lb. chopped almonds

Prepare the fruit the day before cake is to be made. Blanch and chop the almonds, remove sugar from the cherries and the mixed peel.

Chop the remainder of the fruit into uniform-sized pieces. Sprinkle with half the brandy, whisky or sherry. Line an 8-inch round or square tin with two thicknesses of brown paper then two of white paper, extending the paper one inch above the level of the tin. Beat the butter and both sugars to a soft cream. Add the unbeaten eggs one at a time, beating well after each addition. Add half the fruit and then the remainder of the brandy. Sift the flour with the spices, baking powder and salt, and add half to the mixture. Add the rest of the fruit and then the remainder of the flour. Place in prepared tin in lower half of oven and bake at a temperature of 275° to 300°F. for 3 to 3½ hours.

Wedding Cake

The rich mixture used for wedding cakes needs time to age or mature in order to develop its best flavour. For this reason it is recommended that the cake be made at least 6 weeks before the wedding.

Keep it wrapped to retain the moistness, but don't ice it at this stage.

Put the almond covering on after a month's storage, store another week and allow yourself about one week to ice and decorate it.

The chart on page 134 gives the ingredients needed for various sizes of wedding cakes, beginning with a ½-lb. butter weight and ending with a 2-lb. mixture (this is recommended for the three-tiered heart-shaped wedding cake).

Making the Cake

Prepare the fruit the day before the cake is to be baked, chopping it into more or less uniform-sized pieces. Sprinkle with half the brandy and allow to stand overnight. Blanch and chop the almonds.

Prepare the tin by lining it with two thicknesses of brown and two of white paper. The white paper should be on the inside. Make sure the paper fits perfectly, for any creases could spoil the smooth surface of the cooked cake.

Beat the butter and sugar to a soft cream and add the eggs one at a time, beating well after each addition. Add half the fruit, the chopped almonds and the remainder of the brandy.

Sift the flour with the baking powder, spices and salt. Add half to the cake mixture, stir in the remainder of the fruit, then the rest of the sifted flour. Mix thoroughly, adding the Parisian essence if used.

Place in the prepared tin and bake according to the directions given on page 135 under heading "Baking Particulars".

As soon as the cake is removed from the oven it may be sprinkled with a little more brandy. Cool in the tin for about half an hour, then remove and allow to become quite cold. To store, place the cake upside down in the tin in which it was cooked, wrap in several thicknesses of paper and place in a cool, dry cupboard.

INGREDIENTS FOR WEDDING CAKES OF VARIOUS SIZES

Ingredients	½ lb. mixture	1 lb. mixture	1¼ lb. mixture	1½ lb. mixture	1¾ lb. mixture	2 lb. mixture
Raisins	¾ lb.	1½ lb.	1 lb. 14 oz.	2¼ lb.	2 lb. 10 oz.	3 lb.
Currants	½ lb.	1 lb.	1¼ lb.	1½ lb.	1¾ lb.	2 lb.
Almonds	¼ lb.	½ lb.	10 oz.	¾ lb.	14 oz.	1 lb.
Sultanas	¾ lb.	1½ lb.	1 lb. 14 oz.	2¼ lb.	2 lb. 10 oz.	3 lb.
Peel	¼ lb.	½ lb.	10 oz.	¾ lb.	14 oz.	1 lb.
Cherries	¼ lb.	½ lb.	10 oz.	¾ lb.	14 oz.	1 lb.
Butter	½ lb.	1 lb.	1¼ lb.	1½ lb.	1¾ lb.	2 lb.
White sugar	¼ lb.	½ lb.	10 oz.	¾ lb.	14 oz.	1 lb.
Brown sugar	¼ lb.	½ lb.	10 oz.	¾ lb.	14 oz.	1 lb.
Eggs	4	8	10	12	14	16
Sherry, whisky or brandy	4 tablespoons	8 tablespoons	10 tablespoons	12 tablespoons	14 tablespoons	16 tablespoons
Plain flour	10 oz.	1 lb. 4 oz.	1 lb. 9 oz.	1 lb. 14 oz.	2 lb. 3 oz.	2½ lb.
Baking powder	½ level teaspoon	1 level teaspoon	1¼ level teaspoons	1½ level teaspoons	1¾ level teaspoons	2 level teaspoons
Nutmeg	½ level teaspoon	1 level teaspoon	1¼ level teaspoons	1½ level teaspoons	1¾ level teaspoons	2 level teaspoons
Mixed spice	½ level teaspoon	1 level teaspoon	1¼ level teaspoons	1½ level teaspoons	1¾ level teaspoons	2 level teaspoons
Salt	Good pinch	¼ level teaspoon	¼ level teaspoon	½ level teaspoon	½ level teaspoon	½ level teaspoon

Parisian essence: This is an optional ingredient used to colour the cake. Use with care—too much will make the cake mixture bitter. Half a teaspoon is sufficient for a ½ lb. mixture, increasing to no more than about 1½ teaspoons for the 2 lb. mixture.